Meg Cabot

WHO WROTE THAT?

LOUISA MAY ALCOTT

JANE AUSTEN

AVI

JUDY BLUME

BETSY BYARS

MEG CABOT

BEVERLY CLEARY

ROBERT CORMIER

BRUCE COVILLE

ROALD DAHL

CHARLES DICKENS

THEODOR GEISEL

WILL HOBBS

ANTHONY HOROWITZ

GAIL CARSON LEVINE

C.S. LEWIS

ANN M. MARTIN

L.M. MONTGOMERY

PAT MORA

WALTER DEAN MYERS

SCOTT O'DELL

BARBARA PARK

GARY PAULSEN

TAMORA PIERCE

EDGAR ALLAN POE

BEATRIX POTTER

PHILIP PULLMAN

MYTHMAKER:
    THE STORY OF
    J.K. ROWLING

MAURICE SENDAK

SHEL SILVERSTEIN

GARY SOTO

R.L. STINE

EDWARD L.
    STRATEMEYER

E.B. WHITE

LAURA INGALLS
    WILDER

LAURENCE YEP

JANE YOLEN

Meg Cabot

Camille-Yvette Welsch

Foreword by
Kyle Zimmer

CHELSEA HOUSE
PUBLISHERS
An imprint of Infobase Publishing

Meg Cabot

Chelsea House
An imprint of Infobase Publishing
132 West 31st Street
New York NY 10001

Library of Congress Cataloging-in-Publication Data
Welsch, Camille-Yvette.
  Meg Cabot / Camille-Yvette Welsch.
    p. cm. — (Who wrote that?)
  Includes bibliographical references and index.
  ISBN 978-0-7910-9631-4 (acid-free paper) 1. Cabot, Meg—Juvenile
literature. 2. Authors, American—20th century—Biography—Juvenile literature.
3. Authors, American—21st century—Biography—Juvenile literature. I. Title.
  PS3553.A278Z95 2008
  813'.54—dc22
  [B]   2007052213

Chelsea House books are available at special discounts when purchased in bulk quantities for business, associations, institutions, or sales promotions. Please call our Special Sales Department in New York at (212) 967-8800 or (800) 322-8755.

You can find Chelsea House on the World Wide Web at http://www.chelseahouse.com

Text design by Keith Trego and Erika K. Arroyo
Cover design by Keith Trego and Jooyoung An

Printed in the United States of America

Bang EJB 10 9 8 7 6 5 4 3 2 1

This book is printed on acid-free paper.

All links and Web addresses were checked and verified to be correct at the time of publication. Because of the dynamic nature of the Web, some addresses and links may have changed since publication and may no longer be valid.

Table of Contents

FOREWORD BY

KYLE ZIMMER
PRESIDENT, FIRST BOOK   6

1   PRINCESS IN PINK   11

2   A STAR IS BORN   19

3   HOW TO BE POPULAR   29

4   COLLEGE BOUND   41

5   PRINCESS IN THE CITY   51

6   QUEEN OF ROMANCE   61

7   THE PRINCESS AND THE PUBLISHERS   73

8   A CHICK WHO WRITES CHICK LIT   87

9   BEACH BABE   97

10   NEW HORIZONS   107

CHRONOLOGY   114

NOTES   116

WORKS BY MEG CABOT   118

POPULAR BOOKS   120

POPULAR CHARACTERS   122

MAJOR AWARDS   126

BIBLIOGRAPHY   127

FURTHER READING   129

INDEX   131

FOREWORD BY
KYLE ZIMMER
PRESIDENT, FIRST BOOK

HUMANITY IS POWERED by stories. From our earliest days as thinking beings, we employed every available tool to tell each other stories. We danced, drew pictures on the walls of our caves, spoke, and sang. All of this extraordinary effort was designed to entertain, recount the news of the day, explain natural occurrences—and then gradually to build religious and cultural traditions and establish the common bonds and continuity that eventually formed civilizations. Stories are the most powerful force in the universe; they are the primary element that has distinguished our evolutionary path.

Our love of the story has not diminished with time. Enormous segments of societies are devoted to the art of storytelling. Book sales in the United States alone topped $24 billion in 2006; movie studios spend fortunes to create and promote stories; and the news industry is more pervasive in its presence than ever before.

There is no mystery to our fascination. Great stories are magic. They can introduce us to new cultures or remind us of the nobility and failures of our own; inspire us to greatness or scare us to death; but above all, stories provide human insight on a level that is unavailable through any other source. In fact, stories connect each of us to the rest of humanity not just in our own time, but also throughout history.

This special magic of books is the greatest treasure that we can hand down from generation to generation. In fact, that spark in a child that comes from books became the motivation for the creation of my organization, First Book, a national literacy program with a simple mission: to provide new books to the most disadvantaged children. First Book has been at work in hundreds of communities for over a decade. Every year, children in need receive millions of books through our organization, and millions more are provided through dedicated literacy institutions across the United States and around the world. In addition, groups of people dedicate themselves tirelessly to working with children to share reading and stories in every imaginable setting from schools to the streets. Of course, this Herculean effort serves many important goals. Literacy translates to productivity and employability in life and many other valid and even essential elements. But at the heart of this movement are people who love stories, love to read, and want desperately to ensure that no one misses the wonderful possibilities that reading provides.

When thinking about the importance of books, there is an overwhelming urge to cite the literary devotion of great minds. Some have written of the magnitude of the importance of literature. Amy Lowell, an American poet, captured the concept when she said, "Books are more than books. They are the life, the very heart and core of ages past, the reason why men lived and worked and died, the essence and quintessence of their lives." Others have spoken of their personal obsession with books, as in Thomas Jefferson's simple statement: "I live for books." But more compelling, perhaps, is the almost instinctive excitement in children for books and stories.

Throughout my years at First Book, I have heard truly extraordinary stories about the power of books in the lives of children. In one case, a homeless child, who had been bounced from one location to another, later resurfaced—and the only possession that he had fought to keep was the book he was given as part of a First Book distribution months earlier. More recently, I met a child who, upon receiving the book he wanted, flashed a big smile and said, "This is my big chance!" These snapshots reveal the true power of books and stories to give hope and change lives.

As these children grow up and continue to develop their love of reading, they will owe a profound debt to those volunteers who reached out to them—a debt that they may repay by reaching out to spark the next generation of readers. But there is a greater debt owed by all of us—a debt to the storytellers, the authors, who have bound us together, inspired our leaders, fueled our civilizations, and helped us put our children to sleep with their heads full of images and ideas.

WHO WROTE THAT? is a series of books dedicated to introducing us to a few of these incredible individuals. While we have almost always honored stories, we have not uniformly honored storytellers. In fact, some of the most important authors have toiled in complete obscurity throughout their lives or have been openly persecuted for the uncomfortable truths that they have laid before us. When confronted with the magnitude of their written work, we can forget that writers are people. They struggle through the same daily indignities and dental appointments, and they experience the intense joy and bottomless despair that many of us do. Yet, somehow they rise above it all to weave a powerful thread that connects us all. It is a rare honor to have the opportunity that these books provide to share the lives of these extraordinary people. Enjoy.

Meg Cabot, author of The Princess Diaries, poses with a fan at a book signing at Harrod's Department Store in London during Cabot's 2005 tour of the United Kingdom. Cabot wears a tiara, a signature piece, at many of her public appearances.

1

Princess in Pink

IF YOU WALK into a bookstore and see a smiling, slim, dark-haired woman decked out in a pink feather boa and a tiara and surrounded by enchanted teenage girls, chances are you have spied internationally known author Meg Cabot. A self-proclaimed teenage misfit, Cabot has won the hearts of girls the world over with her tales of high-school life, romance, and even paranormal activity.

Cabot has always had stories in her head. As many authors do, she plays the "What if?" game: She asks herself question upon question, which she hopes will help her create a story. When she was small, Cabot used to wonder: What would it be like to be a princess? When will my real parents, the king and queen, claim me? How will they punish my pesky younger brothers for bothering me? How will they punish my parents for disciplining me? As she grew older, she wondered: What if a girl got struck by lightning and received supernatural powers as a result? What if a girl could talk to ghosts, and if she fell in love with one of the ghosts, how could they ever be happy? What if your best friend took a vampire to the prom? These questions are just the tip of the literary iceberg.

An accomplished author in multiple genres, Cabot has written books for many different audiences including girls just entering their teens and adults in search of a fun romance novel or some chick lit. She began writing as a child, when she believed that Barbie and *Star Wars'* Princess Leia deserved longer, better plot lines than were possible in the media in which they originally appeared. As she grew up, Cabot continued to write, although she also found time to read, play with animals, and participate in the theater program at her school. In college, Cabot majored in art, but she took at least one writing class each semester. These classes helped her to become a writer. Cabot learned that not everyone would love her writing and that was okay. She also learned that she might, in fact, have an audience. In every class, a few girls always loved her stories. The workshops reinforced something that her grandmother said, which Cabot often quotes: "You're not a hundred dollar bill. Not everyone is going to like you." More important, Cabot found out that not everyone would like her writing.

After college, Cabot moved to New York City, where she found a job as an assistant director of a residence hall

Did you know...

In a *Wall Street Journal* article dated May 1, 2003, reporter Shelley Branch cites Cabot as the creator of a new linguistic trend.* When a word or phrase that initially has a negative connotation later becomes positive, it is called amelioration. For instance, Michael Jackson made the word *bad* mean *good*, and Paris Hilton has made *hot* refer to a fabulous style instead of temperature. Cabot's contribution comes from her most famous character, Mia Thermopolis (*The Princess Diaries*), who expresses joy, surprise, and disbelief in one little phrase: "Shut-up!" The phrase has caught on among teenagers, and New York stylist Stacey London uses it often on her TLC show, *What Not to Wear*. The usage has become so widespread that the New Oxford American Dictionary may include the new, hip meaning of the phrase in the next edition. In the article, Cabot claims that she heard the phrase from school kids in Manhattan, although some argue that the character Elaine first used it on *Seinfeld*. Nevertheless, Anne Hathaway's portrayal of Mia in the movie relied heavily on the "Shut-up!" exclamation and brought it further into the teenage mainstream.

* Shelley Branch, "Twisting Phrases? Shut-Up!" *Wall Street Journal*, May 1, 2003.

Meg Cabot works while her one-eyed cat, Henrietta, supervises. This photograph was taken in 1996 at the first New York City apartment Cabot shared with her husband.

at New York University. Surrounded by college students and their high-spirited mischief, Cabot gathered dozens of stories and observations that would later appear in her Heather Wells stories (such as *Size 12 Is Not Fat*, *Size 14*

Is Not Fat Either, and *Big Boned*), as well as her other novels. Although she had to deal with everything from grumpy resident advisers to undergraduates who took dangerous risks when they rode atop the dormitory's elevator cars like surfers, Cabot was able to keep focused and return to her writing.

Cabot's first book was finally published in 1998. Since then, she has written more than 50 books and has contributed to a number of anthologies. Her books have been made into movies, television shows, and even manga (Japanese-style comic books). Cabot attributes some of her prolific output to her recently diagnosed hyperactivity, but she also says that part of her success comes from the fact that she just continues to write, regardless of rejection (the first book of The Princess Diaries was rejected 17 times before it was accepted by a publisher). Cabot claims that she feels compelled to write. As other people must paint, play music, or even breathe, she needs to write.

Close observation is necessary in order to write. Cabot advises new writers to listen, eavesdrop on conversations, learn the cadence of speech, and understand how an individual's speech helps to define that person. As a result of Cabot's natural curiosity and tendency to ask questions, stories blossom, usually based around a strong young woman. The women in her stories have specific strengths, weaknesses, and opinions, and each makes her own decisions and faces the consequences. Many of these young women have close friends and families who have helped them to become strong, perhaps because Cabot has been so close to her own friends and family.

People from all over the world view Cabot's blog, so her friendships now have an international flavor. The chatty updates and her profile on MySpace.com have helped to solidify Cabot's image as a friend to girls who feel out of place perhaps because of their appearance, intelligence, or hobbies. Cabot said,

> Basically, my teen years were so horrible, I guess I keep trying to relive them via fiction, and this time actually enjoy them, or get them right. I also think that because I remember how alone and freakish I felt at that time, I hope that by reading my books, other kids who felt like I did will realize they AREN'T alone, that other people have lived through it and survived, and so can they.[1]

Cabot is dedicated to her fans, and she acknowledges readers on her blog with pictures from her book tour appearances and excerpts from letters that have touched her or made her laugh. At the heart of all of these friendships is the exchange of stories. Every time she includes an excerpt of a reader's letter, Cabot teaches her fans to respect their own voices and their own power as storytellers.

In less than a decade, Cabot has published dozens of books, signed thousands of autographs, and embraced youth culture with enthusiasm. An avid fan of television, Cabot chats about the most recent episodes of the latest hot shows, as well as the best young adult fiction. She sponsors a monthly online book club for girls and works with Tamora Pierce on a Web site called Sheroes.com, which promotes and discusses female heroes in literature. She is caretaker to a grumpy one-eyed cat named Henrietta, and she received the ALA Notable Book of the Year award. Her book *The Princess Diaries* (volume 1) was made into two movies, and she wore a glamorous Betsey Johnson dress to the opening for the first. From mangas to blogs, she has embraced the world of technology and the young women who will someday run the world. Cabot, however, was not always the savvy, self-confident author she is today. First, she had to live through high school.

The Cabot family was exceptionally close; Barbara and Vic Cabot made sure that their children were happy and healthy through multiple educational, social, and travel opportunities. The family is shown here in 1973; from left, the children are Nick, Meg, and Matt.

2

A Star Is Born

BARBARA AND VIC Cabot met when they were going to school in Chicago. Barbara Mounsey, a sophomore at Munde-lein College, and A. Victor Cabot, a doctoral student at Northwestern University, went to a mixer. This was an event, often sponsored by a school, where college-aged men and women could meet and socialize. At the social, Vic spied the tall, blue-eyed Barbara and asked her to dance. The mixer was successful for them: They dated for more than two years and were married in 1965, three weeks after Barbara's graduation.

Barbara said of her husband, "I always thought Vic looked a little like Bill Cosby, if Cosby was a white guy. Tall, lanky, balding, with a rather casual dress-code, to say the least (jeans, even to teach)—sometimes he grew a beard, and then he really looked like the classic professor type."[1] The classic professor type was what he became. The couple moved to Bloomington, Indiana, so that Vic could join the faculty at Indiana University. Vic Cabot was a professor of Quantitative Business Analysis at the School of Business at Indiana University.

A little more than a year after they married, Barbara Cabot learned that she was pregnant. One of her college professors had named her daughter Meghan, and Cabot, hearing the name for the first time, thought it was lovely. Later, someone told her that the name should be pronounced "Mee-gan." Barbara did not like the sound of that, so she decided to spell her daughter's name "Meggin" so there would be no doubt as to how to pronounce it. Unfortunately, this also meant that no one could ever find preprinted cups or bracelets with the little girl's full name on them. Meggin Patricia Cabot was born on February 1, 1967.

BABY ON BOARD

As Meg grew up, her parents tried to figure out which traits their daughter had inherited, as most parents do. Vic Cabot taught math and computer science to business students. Although Meg did inherit some other qualities from her father, she did not inherit his talent for math. The difference in their math abilities, as well as Meg's lack of interest in the subject, sometimes caused tension around the house, but their shared sense of humor helped to smooth over the rough spots.

Both Meg and her father shared an outgoing nature. Like his daughter, Vic Cabot was the life of the party. He liked to tell jokes and stories and to make people laugh. According to his wife, the stories about his classroom high jinks, as well as his teaching awards, are still told at Indiana University. Barbara Cabot believes that the humor and comedic timing her daughter would later display at her book readings come from Vic Cabot.

Barbara Cabot blames herself for Meg's lack of math skills. Cabot had little interest in or talent for math, but she did have talent in art. As an illustrator, she introduced Meg to the visual arts, including drawing and painting, as well as the art of writing. Cabot thinks that some of Meg's lighthearted whimsy is a result of the close bond between mother and daughter. In addition, Barbara Cabot herself had some success as a writer: At age 19, she won *Seventeen* magazine's fiction contest. Ironically, Meg later entered this contest several times, but she never won. Finally, Barbara believes she influenced Meg's liberal values and social conscience. For readers of Cabot's blog, those values are pretty clear. Cabot champions tough, strong females, who have the freedom to say what they want, wear what they want, read what they want, and believe what they want. She also believes in the individual's ability to make good, ethical decisions.

The Cabots' new daughter brought them a lot of joy. A son, Matthew, followed three years later. Although they were happy with their family, the Cabots still wanted one more child. They also wanted to make the world a better place and so decided to adopt a child. Meg's youngest brother, Nick, was born in 1972 and came to his adoptive family when he was two months old. The adoption agency thought that Nick's racially mixed heritage (he was the child of African-American and white parents) would make him difficult to place. The Cabots felt that the little boy

Meg gets ready to blow out the candles at her thirteenth birthday party at the Cabots' house in Bloomington, Indiana. Also pictured are Meg's best friends from as far back as fourth grade.

could grow up in their home without racial prejudice, and they believed that both sets of grandparents, aunts, uncles, and cousins would love the boy.

For the most part, the Cabots were right. Both families embraced the boy, although people in the community did not always accept him. In the town, which was centered around the university, the population was varied. Many people were well educated, and the atmosphere was, as Cabot describes it, "quite cosmopolitan and artsy (for Indiana)."[2] Outside the town, the demographics were different: Many people were uneducated and racially intolerant. In fact, Cabot said, "the county next to mine had the highest illiteracy rate in the country for a while."[3] People said cruel things to Nick and their family; once, someone even did so in a church parking lot. Cabot said that was when she realized that just because you went to church and said you were religious, it did not mean you were a good person. Nevertheless, within their home, the family was happy.

The Cabots' hometown of Bloomington, Indiana, had its own attractions. Meg could walk to school, the public pool, the library, and the small downtown area, which was lively. The only place that was beyond walking distance was the mall. Meg and her brothers thrived in Bloomington, where they had their own rooms in the family's 100-year-old farmhouse. As a child, Meg bickered and played with her brothers for hours. They were required to do chores, especially to clean the bathroom that they shared. It was Meg's job to clean the bathtub, and her brothers had to clean the toilet. To ensure that they got the job done, Meg would threaten to tell their parents about whatever mischief her brothers had gotten into during the week.

Meg's room faced the front of the house and featured a large bay window that overlooked the porch roof. Inside her room, everything was feminine. Shelves displayed Madame Alexander dolls and model horses, although she never played with these collections. Instead, she turned her attention to her *Star Wars* action figures and her Barbie dolls. Her mother remembers that some of Meg's first stories were about Princess Leia. Meg wanted more complex stories for the heroine and, when the movies failed to supply them, she wrote them herself. She also wrote elaborate stories in which Barbie became a crime solver as a result of "the brutal serial slaying of the Sunshine Family." Cabot remembered, "Ken was generally the killer."[4]

When Meg was not with her brothers, she spent time with her many friends. The girls would "swim, play street tag, ride bikes and make up stories" using a series of props that included paper dolls, action figures, and Barbies.[5] She also played dress up with her mother's old bridesmaid dresses. Cabot joked that she still does essentially the same things with her friends now, only without the props. She still has the urge to dress up, and she often appears at her book readings bedecked in sparkly tiaras and feather boas.

Did you know...

Barbara Cabot revealed that her daughter has always been crazy about animals. The Cabots had a cat named Quasimodo and a dog named Falstaff, and Meg had her own cat that was named Mewsie. Although her parents were fond of literary names, Meg chose names that appealed to her. She named her next cat Genevieve Valbourth, after her grandmother's rival, and she called the cat Jenny. When Meg moved from Indiana to New York City, Jenny moved with her and lived to be 23 years old! Now, as many readers of her blog know, Cabot and her husband have two cats, one-eyed Henrietta and the cat who adopted them, Gem. Cabot's husband named Gem because, he said, she was a little gem. Cabot was less enamored of the name.

BOOKWORM

Perhaps one of the most valuable lessons her parents taught Meg was to love and value reading. When she was young, the Cabots spent a lot of time reading to their small daughter. She loved the books about Frances, particularly *Bedtime for Frances* and *A Baby Sister for Frances*, and they were delighted that she understood the subtle humor in the books. They read the "Madeline" books until the spines cracked and the pages were smudged with fingerprints. Meg also fell in love with fairy tales, especially "Beauty and the Beast." Clearly, this early exposure to princesses and fairy tales would serve her well; as a writer, one of her most popular characters is a princess.

On vacations, the Cabot family often visited the grandparents in Florida and Colorado, both long drives from the Midwest. When Meg was 14, the family went on their most exciting vacation. Meg had entered and won a drawing contest sponsored by Sears, and along with 50 other winners and their families, the Cabots enjoyed superstar treatment at Disneyland in California.

Although vacations were not always as delightful as Disneyland, holidays were a big deal at the Cabot household. Barbara decorated trees and baked cookies for Christmas, colored and dyed eggs for Easter, created costumes for Halloween, wore green for St. Patrick's Day, and made cards for Valentine's Day. Vic Cabot was less interested in the holidays, an outlook that he passed on to his children, although Cabot's Key West house sports a pink flamingo on top of the Christmas tree. For birthday parties, the Cabot children were permitted to invite guests equal in number to their new age. When she turned nine, Meg invited nine friends for her very first sleepover party. Barbara remembers that the girls talked and giggled all

Above is a basketball game at Indiana. While Meg did not attend any games while she was at Indiana, she did use the money from selling her complimentary student tickets to buy printer ink so she could print out her short stories.

night, and they barely slept at all. Some of these good times would show up in Meg Cabot's books about female friendship.

In order to build a strong moral foundation and instill a sense of core values, the Cabots went to church as a family. Although Meg Cabot no longer attends church, her mother thinks she benefited from the hours the family spent there.

In the Cabot house, the children were expected to work together, and each child had chores. They were required to clean the bathroom, set the table, load and unload the dishwasher, and put the dishes away. As a result, they bickered endlessly over whose turn it was to do each chore. Despite their squabbling, the Cabot children were learning valuable life skills. Barbara also taught her children to do their own laundry. When Meg entered college, she was one of the few freshmen who actually knew how to wash her own clothes.

Life for Meg was easygoing and fun, which allowed her the time, space, and confidence to develop her own thoughts and stories. From the very beginning, Meg's family supported her interest in writing and reading. Meg's daily walks to the library and all the time she spent reading would have amazing results.

Every year, Meg Cabot's grandparents would send her a doll for her birthday. On her sixteenth birthday, Meg decided that the collectible "Sasha" doll she received (shown here) would be the last.

3

How to
Be Popular

ALTHOUGH THE FAMILY'S permanent home was in Bloomington, Indiana, the Cabots moved around a bit when Meg was a child because her father received regular time off. As a professor, Victor Cabot could apply for a sabbatical year to pursue his research interests. Universities give professors this time so that they can conduct research or write books and articles within their discipline, or lecture or work as a visiting professor at another school.

Meg learned to read and write English during the year the Cabot family spent in France. Although the language around her was French, Barbara encouraged Meg to write stories in

English. Later, when she was 13, the family spent a year in California, where Meg attended Junipero Serra Mission School in Carmel. This became the setting for the Mediator series, although Cabot concedes that the place is much changed in her book. First, Cabot's school was an elementary school that ended at the eighth grade, in contrast to the mission high school featured in the book. Second, as far as Cabot knows, the school is not haunted. Nevertheless, no matter where she was, she continued to read and write.

Cabot attributes much of her success to good teachers, and she cares enough to name them. In the third grade, Miss Mize supported her writing, and in the fourth and fifth grades it was Mrs. Hunter at Elm Heights. In the eighth grade, her teacher at the Mission School, Mr. Dan Gotch, told her that writers can write anywhere, even from jail. Meg took it to heart and continued to write wherever she was. This may explain why she likes to write from bed.

As a freshman in high school, Meg received an honor from her teacher, Mr. Mann, who read one of her stories to the class. In an e-mail interview, Cabot said, "I guess it was pretty memorable because a guy I saw recently from that class STILL remembered the story, over twenty years later. That kind of freaked me out."[1]

Perhaps Cabot should not have been surprised to have a classmate remember her story. She remembers her own favorite stories and passes along those names and authors through her Web site. As a child, she enjoyed comic books, particularly *Star Wars* and *Spider-man*, as well as Betty and Veronica from the *Archie* comics. Meg also enjoyed science fiction and fantasy novels. She spent hours in the air-conditioned Monroe County Library, absorbed in the books of Ursula K. LeGuin, Isaac Asimov, Piers Anthony, Susan Cooper, Lloyd Alexander, John Christopher, Judy Blume, Paula Danzinger, and Madeline L'Engle.[2] These books helped her to learn plotting and characterization, techniques she began using in the fledgling novels she wrote during junior high and high school. These books also reinforced for her the idea that reading, while educational, can also be purely pleasurable.

In addition to her novels, Meg kept journals in which she wrote feverishly. Much of her journal-writing was taken up with the subject of boys. Today, Cabot uses those records to help her capture the voice of teenagers and the issues they face.

BOY CRAZY

Meg's interest in the opposite sex started in the fifth grade, when she developed a crush on a redheaded boy who loved snakes and had a wicked sense of humor. The teacher asked Meg to sit next to the boy in class, hoping that she would be a good influence. The plan backfired, as Meg "fell as deeply in love with him as a fifth grader CAN fall in love.[3] During a field trip to a local skating rink, the boy asked 10-year-old Meg to skate as a couple, which thrilled her. Unfortunately, the childhood romance did not continue—the boy moved to Wisconsin. Cabot used the experience in her book *When Lightning Strikes*, as inspiration for the situation when Jess sits next to Rob to be a good influence. She revised history, though; this time, the boy stays and the seating plan sparks a more lasting relationship.

Meg also found companionship and fun when she joined after-school theater groups. At age 13, while in California, she starred in a holiday production by a community children's theater. She painted sets and rehearsed after school and on weekends. In an interview, Barbara Cabot recalled that Meg really liked the camaraderie and team-work necessary for a good production. The theater crowd helped her to make friends, regardless of which school she was attending at the time. Cabot has said that the theater people were the ones with whom she wanted to be friends. She admired their flamboyant ways and all the fun they seemed to have together.

Consistent with the average-girl persona that Cabot later developed, she shared the details of her young adulthood. One of these theater productions led to her first kiss. Nervous before heading onstage, she was stunned when a boy in the show grabbed her and kissed her. Meg was in shock, but she came to a decision: If he liked her enough to kiss her like that, then maybe she could like him back. Her resolve lasted until a girlfriend approached her excitedly and told her that the very same boy had just kissed her. The friend wanted to know if Meg thought that meant he liked her. They realized the boy had kissed every girl in the play, but instead of getting jealous of each other, the girls stuck together and got mad at the boy. After all, he was the one who caused all the trouble. This early example of girl power stayed with Cabot and influenced the characters in her books.

CULT OF POPULARITY

Meg was not always lucky with all of her friends. As a young child, she befriended a neighbor, and the two girls spent a lot of time together. Both were very imaginative and bright, and Barbara Cabot remembers that "they played endless games of Barbie adventures, and then they

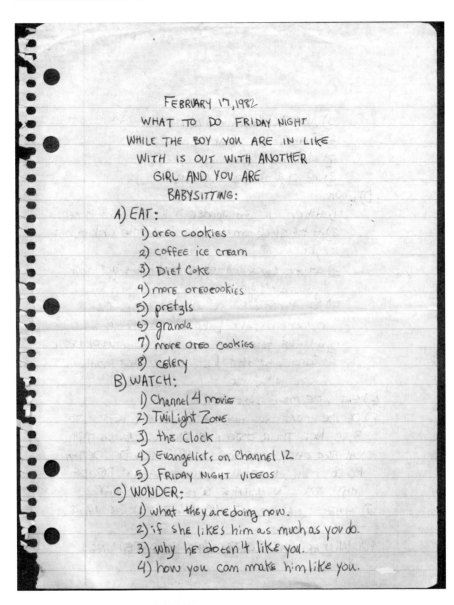

FEBRUARY 17, 1982
WHAT TO DO FRIDAY NIGHT
WHILE THE BOY YOU ARE IN LIKE
WITH IS OUT WITH ANOTHER
GIRL AND YOU ARE
BABYSITTING:
A) EAT:
   1) oreo cookies
   2) coffee ice cream
   3) Diet Coke
   4) more oreo cookies
   5) pretzls
   6) granola
   7) more oreo cookies
   8) celery
B) WATCH:
   1) Channel 4 movie
   2) Twilight Zone
   3) the Clock
   4) Evangelists on Channel 12
   5) FRIDAY NIGHT VIDEOS
C) WONDER:
   1) what they are doing now.
   2) if she likes him as much as you do.
   3) why he doesn't like you.
   4) how you can make him like you.

Reproduced above is a page from Meg Cabot's childhood journal.

fell under the Star Wars spell, and played Princess Leia in
outer space all the time, and were in Girl Scouts together,
and it all came to a crashing end when they got to middle

school, and the little neighbor girl discovered cheerleaders and boys and popularity." The girl dumped Meg, which made her feel betrayed and angry.

Even as a child, Meg never bought into the cult of popularity, and she stays true to this message in her young adult books. Her protagonists are usually outside the social mainstream, and they are happy to avoid the popular crowd and their idea of exclusivity within a clique. Even those who yearn for popularity find the reality much less fulfilling

Did you know...

Cabot is a dedicated philanthropist. She gives to numerous causes, including the American Society for Prevention of Cruelty to Animals (ASPCA) and the Campaign to End Fistula. She also encourages readers to do what they can to make the world a better place. Her Web site has dedicated a page to acknowledging good works, both those of Cabot and her readers. During her tour for *Princess Diaries VI*, Cabot decided to use her fame to help the less fortunate. She asked her readers to bring gently used prom dresses to readings. All of the dresses would go to The Cinderella Affair, an organization in Tempe, Arizona, that provides a prom dress "boutique" for young women who cannot afford a brand-new gown. Cabot praised her readers in her blog, as dozens of dresses were collected for the charity. Cabot again illustrated her desire to make every girl feel like a princess.

than the dream. Despite Meg's breakup with her neighbor, she found solace in other friends, girls who would become famous as the inspiration for characters in her novels. (Today, Meg and her neighbor have made up and become close friends again.)

Cabot explains that some of her characters are based on friends who inspired her:

> I had lots of best friends, most of whom are still my best friends now. I had a dreamy, romantic friend, who was still very practical about boys—and still is today—who became the inspiration for Tina Hakim Baba in the Princess Diaries series, and a funny, smart, sarcastic friend who became the inspiration for Lilly Moscovitz (actually, she is a mix of several friends who are all smart and sarcastic). I had a sweet overweight friend who became the inspiration for Becca in *How to Be Popular* and also Ruth in the 1-800-Where-R-You series, and a whip smart friend who happened to be albino who became the inspiration for CeeCee in the Mediator series. We all still exchange holiday cards and email often, and I often see them when I'm on book tour. Some of them I call so frequently they answer the phone going, "What NOW?"[4]

Although Meg had a lot of female friends, she was also interested in boys. As a teenager, Meg used the large bay window in her bedroom as an escape route. She would climb out the window, across the roof and down into the front yard, where she would creep across neighbors' lawns to meet her boyfriend in the empty yard of a nearby house for sale. This appears in her books, as Suze from the Mediator series and Jess from the 1-800-Where-R-You series often sneak away to either visit their boyfriends or deal with some official ghost or missing persons business.

Meg attended two proms in high school, although her memories are not entirely good. She bought her dresses with babysitting money and then asked her mom to alter them to make them more stylish. Her date to the first prom was a boy she really liked. Unfortunately, she already had a boyfriend, who was out of town during the prom. The news got back to her boyfriend's mom, who lectured Meg about her decision, and to his friends, who yelled at her, too. According to Meg's logic, she was the wronged party, since the boyfriend was the one who decided to leave town during prom. Although she did go to the prom, neither boy forgave her deception, and both boys broke up with her shortly thereafter.

The second prom was a similar debacle, only this time Meg's date had a girlfriend at another school, and Meg was the one who found out about it later. These experiences contributed to Cabot's belief that no one has fun at his or her prom. In fact, Cabot later wrote about proms with other young adult authors in *Prom Nights From Hell*. The kids in her story have bigger problems than missing significant others: They have problems with vampires.

In addition to chasing boys, Meg did a lot of baby-sitting. From 1980 to 1985, she worked as a child-care assistant for well-known feminist scholar Susan Gubar, who studies women and literature. Gubar published famous books of literary criticism and feminist theory; the most famous one is *The Madwoman in the Attic*. Perhaps the ideas of her employer influenced Meg, who considers herself a staunch feminist. Feminists believe that women should have equal access to education, equal protection under the law, equal educational and recreational opportunities, and equal pay for equal work. Essentially, they believe that women should be afforded the same rights as men and that the oppression

Meg Cabot found a circle of friends and a passion when she began participating in theater productions at school. Above, she poses with a friend in her costume as the character Daisy Mae in the musical Li'l Abner. Incidentally, the young man in this photo was one of Meg's prom dates.

of the past, when women were considered to be property or treated like children, must end.

Meg really enjoyed the kids for whom she baby-sat. Unfortunately, once the children became too old for baby-sitters, she had to move on. She tried to work at Rax Roast Beef, but she only lasted three long days, which she blamed on the uniform (green polyester pants and a visor) and the sneezing on the salad bar. Then she began to work at the Viewpoint Bookstore, a job she had throughout college. The bookstore, now closed, sat on Courthouse Square in downtown Bloomington, Indiana.

TALL, DARK, AND INFURIATING?

The proximity of Indiana University also played a part in Meg's life, not only because of her famous employer Dr. Gubar, but also because of her boyfriend. When Meg was sixteen, she dated a boy who was in college. The couple dated on and off for years. They were at a party when her boyfriend introduced her to his friend, a tall, dark-haired 22-year-old student named Benjamin Egnatz. The two started to talk, and Meg told him that she wanted to be a writer. Egnatz told Meg that she should not study creative writing at the university. As an English major, he felt that all the joy had gone out of writing as a result of his major. He joked to her boyfriend that Meg needed a baby-sitter and teased her about her curfew. Although she took his advice about the major, Meg did not like Egnatz very much. This would change when she encountered him again years later in New York City.

Meg also spent a lot of her time on her schoolwork. In her senior year of high school, Meg found great support for her writing from two teachers, Mrs. Granich and Mr. Beaver, each of whom helped Meg meet her literary as-pirations. Although she excelled in all language-oriented subjects, math baffled Meg. She remembers how difficult it was to multiply and divide algebraic fractions, and how that was a source of particular vexation for her father. He felt that she should master the concepts; Meg was con-vinced she would never need the skills. She claims she was right in the end, although the numbers started to make sense once she could apply them to real people and real payrolls. Cabot later used her mathematical awakening as a detail in her book *How to Be Popular* when her character, Steph Landry, has to handle the payroll for her mother's bookstore. Unfortunately, Meg did not master math in time for the SAT exams. She scored in the low 400s out of a possible 800 on the math section, which she believed was going to make it very difficult to get into college.

Indiana University admitted Meg, though, and because her father was a professor there, her education was free. In Meg's mind, this made her free to take seemingly impractical classes. Her first problem was to decide on a major. She had loved animals all of her life, and had many pets; even now, Cabot has pets who she frequently mentions in her blog. Veterinarians have to take a lot of courses in science and math, both of which Meg found painful and difficult. English major Ben Egnatz had told her not to take English, and so she returned to another love, the one that had won the family a trip to Disneyland. Meggin Cabot enrolled in Indiana University in 1985 as an art major.

After college, Meg Cabot (above) and her boyfriend moved to New York City. Cabot's mother was worried about her daughter's safety; at the time, New York was considered to be a dangerous city.

4

College Bound

WHEN CABOT LEFT for college, she loved Madonna and liked to dress all in black. She modeled herself after the singer, who was in her "nutty/slutty" stage (as described by Barbara Cabot).[1] That meant fingerless lace gloves, bustiers, and lots of jewelry: Madonna as she appeared in *Desperately Seeking Susan*. Despite what others may have thought of her appearance, Cabot was a serious student headed to college. As a result of her father's position at Indiana University, Cabot could go to school for free, and she took advantage of the opportunity. She majored in art, and took classes in drawing and painting, sculpture and ceramics. The classes were fun, and Cabot could pursue them guilt-free and loan-free. Yet, in the midst of all the fun art classes, Cabot still made time for writing classes.

Indiana University is a large state school with nearly 40,000 students at the Bloomington campus. With beautiful white gates at the school's entrance, the campus boasts 1,860 acres and the thirteenth-largest library in North America. It is a lovely and historic campus, and some of the buildings are even on the National Historic Registry. Indiana has lots of sports fans in the student body and is known not only for academics and athletics, but for social opportunities, as well.

When Cabot was in school, Indiana University had one of the largest and oldest Greek systems in the country. Young men and women would pledge a particular fraternity or sorority, and after a series of interviews and entrance activities, the fraternity would decide either to admit or decline the pledge. For many people, membership in a fraternity leads to lifelong friends, but others believe that the fraternity system lets you buy your friends with fraternity dues. Cabot was never impressed with the Greek system and saw it as just another popularity contest sanctioned by the school. She also thought it was ridiculous to live in a house full of women when she could live in a coed dorm.

In addition to these reasons, Cabot had also had some experience with the fraternities. When Cabot was in high school, her mother kept plants on their front porch. One morning, the plants went missing and were later found on the front porch of one of the fraternity houses, whose members had stolen them for their own use. The bad behavior continued when Cabot entered college. One fraternity had painted a sidewalk with the words, "Fat Chicks Go Home." Even worse, the boys would gather on the porch of their house and raise scorecards as women went by. The cards rated women's appearances on a scale of 1 to 10.[2] A disgusted Cabot took another route to class, although those fraternity boys are featured in her Heather Wells series, in which dorm assistant Heather Wells solves the mystery surrounding the deaths of several college students. The fraternities at Indiana University, together with the students at New York University, helped Cabot to create a realistic and unsavory picture of some fraternities.

LIFE ON CAMPUS

As a freshman, Cabot roomed in the Collins Living Learning Center, a residential dorm that focuses on creating a close-knit, student-centered atmosphere. Students who live in Collins take additional courses through the residence hall, many of which count toward their degree. The courses are offered in the dorm, so students get to know their neighbors better and participate in the arts, service projects, and other unique educational opportunities. Cabot remembered the dorm fondly and said it was "the prettiest, oldest residence hall on campus."[3] During the first year, Cabot roomed with her best friend, and in her second year, she had the freedom of a single room. Each student living in Collins was required to take a course in the dorm. As soon as Cabot saw the list, she knew she would take creative writing. The class changed the way that Cabot thought about writing.

Judy Troy, Cabot's instructor, loved her writing and encouraged her to take some risks. Unlike many teachers, Troy told Cabot to embrace her sense of humor and bring it into her writing. Troy herself went on to become a successful writer; her books include *West of Venus, Mourning Doves*, and *From the Black Hills*. She was the recipient of the prestigious Whiting Writing Award in 1996. Troy helped Cabot see that the act of writing could be fun, and that the writing itself had the potential to be fun. It was a revelation for the budding humor writer: She did not have to write serious fiction to be taken seriously.

Troy's class was just the beginning. With the confidence she gained from Troy's instruction, Cabot took more classes. In fact, Cabot took a creative writing class every semester. In the back of her mind, she kept the words of a certain older man in mind. Ben Egnatz had told her that the

Did you know...

In an article in the *Wall Street Journal* dated June 20, 2006, Cabot revealed that success is the best revenge. She claims that many people come to her readings and bring their daughters to meet Cabot. Some of these mothers were the mean girls from high school, and they often claim to have been friends with Cabot, although she remembers it a bit differently.

creative writing program would make her hate writing, and that it would suck all the joy and mystery out of reading and writing. Although Cabot did not pursue creative writing as a major, she also could not stay away from the lure of words.

Cabot also enjoyed her other classes. She had always worked hard in school and generally excelled, and college was no different. The courses offered her new perspectives, new interests, and new teachers. Unfortunately, she still did battle with math, her old demon, but with the help of dedicated professors, she also passed her math classes. Cabot, however, was not partnered solely with her books; she had other interests that compelled her.

IF I CAN MAKE IT THERE. . . .

Cabot's dating life was active in college, as it was in high school, even if it was mostly with the same boy. Barbara said that some of the boys Meg Cabot dated became characters in her books and that Cabot's sharp eye for detail makes the ex-boyfriends easily recognizable and easily identifiable based on their bad behavior.[4]

By the end of college, Cabot and her boyfriend were engaged to be married, and they planned to move to New York City. Barbara said that she was terrified to have her daughter move to the big city. New York City during the 1980s was very different from the way it is now. Murder rates were high, as were burglaries and other violent crimes. Times Square used to be a seedy place, rife with adult movie theaters and bookstores. The city began to turn around in the early 1990s, particularly after Rudy Giuliani became mayor. He put new crime-fighting technology into effect, and the city's crime wave began to reverse itself. As of 2007, New York City had one of the lowest murder rates of any major city in the United States. In 1989, however, Barbara Cabot seemed to have good reason to worry.

Nevertheless, the summer after college, the Cabots helped pack up their daughter's belongings and sent her off to New York City, where Meg Cabot hoped to find work as a freelance illustrator. Barbara had long worked as a freelance illustrator, where she provided illustrations for various businesses and organizations. Meg Cabot, armed with her portfolio, was ready to take New York by storm. Unfortunately, New York was unmoved by Cabot's efforts.

Cabot has said that she dropped off her portfolio at numerous businesses, such as Condé Nast (a magazine publisher), MTV magazine, and Planned Parenthood, where her mother had worked. After several weeks, she began to get a real sense of the competition she faced and the bills that she would have to pay if she wanted to remain in the city. Things became tense, and Cabot needed to find a way to support herself in her new life. The choice that she made led her on another adventure.

DORM DIVA

After she looked at a number of jobs, Cabot decided to apply for the position of assistant manager at a New York University dorm. She had spent much of her teenage years as a baby-sitter, and it seemed that the job would be similar, only for freshman college students. She would hold their hands at the hospital when they were sick, defuse roommate disputes, comfort forlorn survivors of unrequited love, and listen to all of the wonderful stories around her. She also organized and hired student workers. On a more

While looking for work as a freelance illustrator, Cabot took a job as an assistant manager at a dormitory at New York University. Every year the university rents Washington Square Park as a space in which to hold the university-wide graduation ceremonies, as shown in this photograph.

practical note, the job was a mere two blocks from her apartment, which saved Cabot both time and money in transportation costs.

The job had other perks, as well. When the students were calm and the dorm was quiet, Cabot could write. She filled page after page with funny, astute prose. Eventually, the pages became stories, and the stories became full-blown novels, but Cabot still considered writing a hobby.

RETURN OF TALL, DARK, AND HANDSOME

In addition to writing, Cabot found new friends, one of whom she had met before. The English student to whom she had reacted so negatively in high school was back in her life. Meg's fiancé was still friends with Benjamin Egnatz, and this time around, Cabot found herself intrigued by the 28-year-old graduate student. Egnatz wrote poetry, but despite their differences as writers, the two found they had much in common: a love of the city, its bustle, its fabulous food, and its seething atmosphere of change. Both shared a great sense of humor and a deep love for television, although they did not always like the same shows. The two became close friends in spite of Cabot's engagement to someone else.

Eventually, her engagement ended. Cabot does not reveal her fiancé's name, or the circumstances of the breakup. In an interview, she said, "I am not going to answer [questions about the relationship] on the grounds that the person in question and I are still friends—and I've kept it that way by keeping what happened out of print."[5] In another interview, however, Cabot suggests that her boyfriend's lack of understanding for her need to write might have led to the breakup.[6] This was not a problem in her relationship with Egnatz.

By the time Cabot was 24, she and Egnatz had begun to date and share tasty dinners, bad television shows, and the compulsion to write. Two years later, they decided on a creative April Fool's Day joke, one that would change their lives forever.

When Ben Egnatz and Meg Cabot decided to elope, they wanted to do so in an intensely romantic place like Italy. They ended up in Liguria, the coastal town shown above.

5

Princess in the City

THE APRIL FOOL'S Day joke started with a fight between Cabot and Egnatz. He wanted to leave some of his things at Cabot's studio apartment, which was essentially a one-room apartment, with a small kitchen and a bathroom. Cabot replied that she would only allow him to keep stuff at her tiny apartment if they were married. The two then decided to take the plunge and get married. Unfortunately (or fortunately, depending on whom you ask), Cabot never cared for the pomp and circumstance of weddings. She did not like the yards of tulle, the plans, or the wedding registry. Instead, she and Egnatz decided to elope to Italy on April Fool's Day.

Egnatz and Cabot liked the idea that they could send postcards home that proclaimed their marriage, dated April 1. The best part would be that no one would know whether or not the postcards were true until they arrived home. They liked the joke and they liked the idea of marrying in an intensely romantic place like Italy.

The two went to Diano San Pietro in Liguria, along the Italian Riviera. The Italian courthouse officials did not want to marry them. They asked Cabot and Egnatz why they could not just get married in Las Vegas like other Americans. After they convinced the mayor that they were serious, he told them that they would have to drive to Milan to get the license. The couple drove to the city and back the next day, receiving two speeding tickets along the way. As a final touch of support, the locals nailed two bedroom slippers to a tree for luck, a bridal tradition in Italy, and decorated the gates with flowers.

APRIL FOOLS

When April 1 dawned, the local children came to the couple's room and knocked on the door. A disheveled Cabot answered and cracked the door to see mournful faces staring up at her. Worried, Cabot asked what was wrong, and the children sadly told her that the mayor had said the two could not be married. Near tears, Cabot thanked them and moved to shut the door, when the children broke into a chorus of "April Fools!" Cabot liked the joke so much she asked them to repeat it for Egnatz, who had been in the shower at the time.

When the couple arrived at the courthouse, the mayor, who wore his soccer-refereeing outfit, awaited them.

He put his robes on over his jersey to perform the ceremony. The town brought flowers for Cabot and helped the couple celebrate with a brunch. Cabot enjoyed her wedding and the Italian people so much that she used the story as a basis for one of her adult novels, *Every Boy's Got One*. Cabot decided that to keep the story interesting, it had to be about someone other than the bride and groom, so she opted for the maid of honor and the best man. Like Cabot and Egnatz, they take an immediate dislike to each other, but they go with their friends to Italy to support their marriage. The wedding hits a number of bumps in the road, which the maid of honor and best man, a reluctant couple, are asked to solve. During the process, they fall in love with each other, and all of the action is communicated via journal, PDA, and e-mail entries. Maid of Honor Holly writes:

> This is going to work. This HAS to work. I know Cal doesn't think it's going to (big surprise). But what does HE know? He's been against those two getting together since before any of this even started. Look at him now, asking for the key to the men's room. He STILL looks as if he doesn't know quite what hit him.[1]

Although there are some substantial differences between fact and fiction, many of the details are the same. As is so often the case, fact inspires great fiction.

When Cabot and Egnatz returned home, everyone was pleased that the postcards had been true. Both sides liked their new family members and welcomed them with open arms. The families gathered to celebrate the union on the back porch of the Cabot home in Indiana. A tornado derailed the celebration a bit, but the revelers trooped on with sweaters and good spirits. Unfortunately, the joy of the wedding was quickly followed by an event of deep sorrow.

DEVASTATING NEWS

Cabot's father, Vic, was battling squamous cell cancer. This particular cancer begins in the squamous cells, which Webster's New World Dictionary defines as "thin, flat cells that resemble fish scales. Squamous cells are found in the tissue that forms the surface of the skin, the lining of the hollow organs of the body, and the passages of the respiratory and digestive tracks."[2] The cancer attacks those cells. Vic Cabot had been ill for some time,

Did you know...

Cabot's father unwittingly inspired her interest in romance writing. He bought her a satirical romance novel, *Generic Romance*, at the grocery store as a joke. His daughter laughed along with him until she read the book and absolutely fell in love with the romance genre. Now, Cabot firmly vows never to make fun of people for what they read.

and the cancer progressed aggressively. He lost his battle soon after his daughter married. Barbara Cabot talked about the death of her husband, explaining, ". . . even though we hoped he would recover, I think we all had a sense of foreboding. Each of us said what we needed to say to him, had let him know how much we loved him."[3] In spite of the time the family was able to spend together, Vic's death still hit Cabot hard. Her fun-loving father, the jokester and mathematical genius, was no longer a phone call or a visit away. Barbara reflected on the effect the death had on her daughter:

> It was hard for Meg, even though she was a grown-up when he died—she had lots of times after he died when she thought she would see him on the street, or had dreams about him. Although we are not very religious, I think all of us feel like a part of him is with us, or we think of him being in the Great Hereafter rooting for the Cubbies and reading a spy novel and seeing what we are doing. And making jokes. The main thing is that time is the great healer . . . everyone tells you that, and it sounds like a cliché, but it is very true.[4]

For Cabot, the death haunted her a little, as her mother noted. She would turn corners and imagine her father in the crowd. In an interview for a Web site called Laurie Likes Books, Cabot talked about her experience after her father's death. She said,

> My brother and I were talking one day, and he mentioned that he kept thinking he saw our father out of the corner of his eye. Well, the exact same thing had been happening to me! We wondered if everyone who has a death in the family experiences this, and from there it was a natural progression

Although Cabot's family was happy to hear about Meg's marriage, their joy was reserved, as they had recently discovered that Vic Cabot was suffering from cancer. Vic Cabot, pictured above with Barbara, died that year.

to: 'Man, what if you could see the ghosts of every dead person?'[5]

The questions stayed with Cabot, and the "Mediator" series was born.

In this series, first published in 2000, 16-year-old Suze Simon can talk to ghosts, including her dead father and an attractive ghost from centuries past.

> My dad was dead, yeah. But I *did* see him again.
>
> In fact, I probably see him more now than I did when he was alive. When he was alive, he had to go to work most days. Now that he's dead, he doesn't have all that much to do. So I see him a lot. Almost too much, in fact. His favorite thing to do is suddenly materialize when I least expect it. It's kind of annoying.
>
> My dad was the one who finally explained it to me. So I guess, in a way, it's a good thing he did die, since I might never have known, otherwise.[6]

In California after her mother has remarried, Suze lives in an old house and attends the local mission school. The school itself, and much of the geography, is based on Cabot's brief stint in California during one of her father's sabbaticals. At the start of the series, Suze is ready to fight at any given moment. She firmly believes that most issues can be settled with a fistfight. Unfortunately, in both the world of the dead and the living, force is not always the most useful tactic. In order to rid herself of the ghosts, both good and bad, Suze has to work toward either solving their problems or exorcising them. Father Dominic, a fellow mediator of somewhat more peaceful measures, helps her. As Suze progresses through the books, one of the primary things that she learns is how to resolve issues with her brain rather than with her fists.

SUBMISSION MISSION

Although the aftermath of her father's death later inspired the Mediator series, Cabot struggled with the loss. She began to write romance novels once again to help her escape her problems, but she was afraid to try submitting her work for publication. Her husband was a great influence in that area. An aspiring writer himself, Egnatz was in graduate school and would send his own work out for publication. Indeed, he has published poems that he wrote for Cabot, one of which appeared in *Callaloo,* a well-known literary journal. Egnatz urged Cabot not only to continue to write, but also to take the plunge and begin to send her work to agents and publishers.

Cabot took her husband seriously. She sent work out and received dozens of rejections, as most writers do. Undeterred, she also began to research agents. An agent not only helps an author sell the literary work to publishing houses and movie studios, but can also help the author to mature as a writer. As Cabot so often mentions on her blog, she went to an authoritative text on the subject, *Jeff Herman's Guide to Agents, Editors, and Publishers*, to help her find the right agent to act as a coach/cheerleader/salesperson. She found her agent, Laura Langlie, who started to champion her writer to different publishing houses; however, it took time before they got a bite. In the interim, Cabot selected a pen name for her romance novels. She had decided that Meg was not a romantic-sounding name, and chose instead her middle name, Patricia, which she felt was more appropriate for the genre.

More name games were to come: Cabot entered the publishing world as Meg Cabot, Meggin Cabot, Patricia Cabot, and Jenny Carroll. The final name introduced her paranormal series, and it was the name of her beloved, longtime feline companion.

diaries

#1 *NEW YORK TIMES* BESTSELLING AUTHOR
MEG CABOT

*When Meg Cabot was troubled by her mother's developing relationship
with one of Cabot's old teachers, Cabot's friends encouraged her to write a
book about her feelings. From this was born* The Princess Diaries, *perhaps
Cabot's most popular novel to date.*

6

Queen of Romance

FOR FOUR YEARS after Cabot's wedding and her father's death, she continued to write and submit manuscripts. As the rejection letters piled up, she began to feel disillusioned and tired of the whole publishing game. She almost gave up. She found that she might have been able to stop submitting manuscripts, but she could never stop writing. She had used her stories to help her deal with boredom and grief. Writing was central to who she was; just as she had to breathe, she had to write. Nevertheless, the road ahead loomed long into the distance, with no end in sight.

Then, on New Year's Eve 1996, Cabot discovered that she was about to become a bona fide published author. With champagne ready in the refrigerator, Cabot and Egnatz joined friends at their SoHo apartment to celebrate. Back in Indiana, Barbara Cabot was ecstatic and proud that all of her daughter's work was finally going to pay off. Although Barbara was thrilled about her child's success, she was a little sad that Vic Cabot would not be around to share in his daughter's achievement. Nonetheless, Meg Cabot's mother and her grandmother still crowed about the success of the new family author.

ROMANCE WRITER

Cabot's first published book was a historical romance novel, *Where Roses Grow Wild*, published in March 1998. The sequel, *Portrait of My Heart*, followed in 1999. In that same year, Cabot also published *An Improper Proposal*, and then, six months later, *A Little Scandal*. St. Martin's Press published all the books under the name Patricia Cabot. One might wonder how so many books were ready in such a short time: Cabot had been writing for years and had manuscripts in drawers in various states of completion.

The setting of Cabot's historical romances was generally nineteenth-century England, which added to the escapist quality, but the books themselves were written in the voice Cabot was developing. Her novels played on class and sudden changes in fortune, and her female characters were strong, likable women with bold opinions. As a setting, the nineteenth century made sense because during this time women were beginning to gain more rights under the law and assume their proper place as individuals equal to men. This was particularly true after the publication of Mary

Wollstonecraft's 1792 book, *A Vindication on the Rights of Women*, in which she set forth her proposition that women should have equal rights under the law and in the social order. These ideas were revolutionary and much disliked, but there were nevertheless some people who wanted such laws to be enacted and these ideals to be incorporated into their own lives. With Cabot's fondness for independent female characters, it makes sense that her historical fiction would be set in an era in which women could begin to have their own adventures, an era that marked the first wave of feminism.

In 2000, Cabot also began to write historical romances for Pocket Books. For *Lady of Skye*, in which the hero and heroine are physicians in a small Scottish village, Cabot tried her hand at a medical mystery. To make her story more authentic, Cabot worked closely with an epidemiologist, a person who studies the frequency and variants of communicable diseases among certain people and places. Cabot had learned the advantages of asking experts when she was in the sixth grade: She interviewed a forensics detective at her local police station, who answered some questions for her science fair project on fingerprinting. The research technique has served her well over the years.

At the same time that Cabot's romance novels were such a success, Cabot began to investigate other styles of writing. Romance was a lot of fun, but some of the stories in the author's head would not be served by the romance genre. Instead, they were destined to become chick lit or young adult novels. One story in particular sprouted in the author's mind and grew into a huge enterprise, and it all stemmed from her widowed mother's love life and Cabot's own love of royalty.

BIRTH OF A PRINCESS

About a year and a half after Vic Cabot's death, Barbara attended a lecture at Indiana University. A friend had carefully orchestrated the seating, and had placed Barbara next to a kind widower named Ron. Coincidentally, Meg Cabot had been a student in one of Ron's art classes at Indiana University. Sparks flew, and Barbara and Ron began to date. The story may sound familiar to Cabot readers, as it is the impetus for *The Princess Diaries* and the romance between Mia's mother and one of Mia's teachers.

Although Cabot was happy that her mother had found a companion, she was unnerved by the fact that Ron was one of her former teachers. After Cabot discussed it endlessly with her friends, they suggested that she use it in her fiction, if only to free their phone lines. Cabot thought it was a fine idea and settled down to write *The Princess Diaries*. But it was not enough to have a teacher date a parent; this did not offer enough conflict for a whole book. A friend suggested that Cabot write about a princess. Cabot decided to meld the two ideas, and used the conflict that surrounded her mother's relationship with the teacher to amplify Mia's feelings of freakishness after she discovers her heritage.

Cabot often states that people feel self-conscious enough without being very different from their peers. She wondered what might happen if the teens in question had seemingly huge differences, like suddenly discovering royal lineage. In *The Princess Diaries*, protagonist Mia is an average teen when the series begins. She has a close friend, Lilly Moscovitz, and the two have resigned themselves to the fact that they are on the fringe of the popular crowd. Both girls have intellectual leanings and liberal upbringings, and both come from middle-class homes. They call each other nightly to chat, to obsess over global issues and their love lives, and to copy homework answers. When Mia is suddenly blindsided by the news that she comes from royal blood and will be the heir to Genovia, she does not know how to react, and neither does her best friend.

Mia's social status undergoes major revisions. The kids at school are suddenly either much nicer to her or even crueler. The popular girls try to befriend her or backstab her, and the popular boys try to date her to get their names in the newspapers. Mia struggles to figure out who she is. Can she still be the environmentally conscious girl that she was? Is there a place for the outspoken in a genteel kingdom? Can she keep her best friend? Will every pimple be magnified on the covers of newspapers the world over? Mia writes in her journal after she is suddenly discovered by the press as a lost royal princess:

> I guess I should have my picture on the front of the *Post* more often. Suddenly I am very popular. I walked into the cafeteria (I told Lars to keep five paces behind me at all times; he kept stepping on the backs of my combat boots), and Lana Weinberger, of all people, came up to me while I was in the jet line getting my tray, and said, "Hey Mia. Why don't you come and sit with us?"
>
> I am not even kidding. That lousy hypocrite wants to be friends with me now that I am a princess.[1]

Mia suddenly gets a new social status, but she also inherits family members, growing closer to her father, the Prince of Genovia, and to her regal and distant grandmother, the Queen of Genovia. Her grandmother endeavors to change Mia both inside and out: She cuts her hair, improves her posture, outfits her with a new wardrobe, and monitors her speech. Outspoken Mia must change to accommodate the demands of her birthright, but Genovia and her people find that they too must change to accept their newly found princess.

Originally, Cabot had thought that Mia's story might be an amusing novel for adults. Granted, it was about a child, but Cabot still thought that adults might like to look back at teenage life. When Cabot's agent read the manuscript, she told Cabot that it was a young adult novel. Her pronouncement was a little eerie for Cabot because of a phone call she had received a few months before.

When Cabot originally conceived of Mia, she kept her work quiet. It seemed as though the character had come fully formed into her head, and she did not want to mess with the magic. She did not even tell her husband. One day, her mother-in-law called and asked if Cabot was writing a young adult novel. Taken aback, Cabot immediately confirmed that she was, and then asked what had spurred the question. Her mother-in-law said that she had been to see a psychic who had told her that her daughter-in-law in New York was writing a young adult book, and that it was going to be very successful. Cabot was not sure how to take the news, but the strange coincidence lit a fire in her, and she hurried to complete the manuscript and give it to her agent.

REJECTION AND REJOICING

Once Cabot's agent, Laura Langlie, got the manuscript, things still were not easy. *The Princess Diaries* was rejected 17 times, but Langlie continued to pitch the book to publishers and even to movie agents. Bill Contardi, then at William Morris Agency, agreed to represent the film rights. Walt Disney Pictures optioned it on behalf of Whitney Houstion's production company, Brownhouse. The agent had heard that

JULIE ANDREWS ANNE HATHAWAY

She needs the rock to rule.

WALT DISNEY
PICTURES PRESENTS
A GARRY MARSHALL FILM · T H E ·
PRINCESS
DIARIES 2
ROYAL ENGAGEMENT
FROM THE DIRECTOR OF 'PRETTY WOMAN' & 'PRINCESS DIARIES'

One way for authors to become very successful is to option the movie rights to their books. Disney bought the rights to The Princess Diaries *and transformed the book into two movies starring Anne Hathaway and Julie Andrews, as shown in the movie poster above.*

Disney wanted to do a film with a girl as the protagonist (main character), and Langlie thought it might be a good fit.

The book finally sold to publisher Avon (which was later purchased by HarperCollins). Then Cabot heard even more stunning news: Disney had optioned the rights for the movie even before the book was published. Now Cabot could quit her job at New York University and concentrate exclusively on writing. Suddenly, Cabot could support

Did you know...

Kaavya Viswanathan, a 19-year-old student at Harvard University, had received a large advance from Little, Brown and Company for her chick-lit book, *How Opal Mehta Got Kissed, Got Wild, and Got a Life*. Shortly after publication, it was discovered that large passages of the book had been plagiarized, taken entirely from the books of other authors, among them Meg Cabot. The publishing company immediately dropped her contract and stopped publication on the book. Cabot, although she does not approve of the behavior, expressed sympathy in an interview with the *Straits Times*, "I feel bad for Kaavya because I think she was a kid and was under enormous pressure. She got this huge advance based on an outline and she didn't actually have a book at the time . . . I feel sorry for her because, not that her life is over, but certainly her writing career is."* The fact that Cabot can acknowledge the mistake, forgive the person, and respect that decisions have consequences is part of what makes her fiction so powerful for young women.

* Kristina Tom, "Living Her Dream," *Strait Times* (Singapore) June 11, 2006.

herself on writing alone, which is a colossal achievement for a writer; in fact, it only happens to a select few.

Published in 2000, *The Princess Diaries* was an immediate success, which pleased Cabot, as she had conceived of the book as the beginning of a series that would follow Mia from her freshman year in high school through to her senior year. The books already had a following, which was further cemented when the American Library Association bestowed two honors upon the novel. It was awarded a Best Book 2000 and a Top Ten Book for Reluctant Readers. Since then, the book has been sold in 38 other countries and Anne Hathaway, the actress who portrayed Mia in the movie version, has narrated the first three audio books.

When Disney optioned the movie, the story underwent a makeover: Mia's father, the Prince of Genovia, was cut from the story. This was presumably to make more screen time for the Queen of Genovia, played by Julie Andrews, who was famous for her leading roles in *Mary Poppins* and *The Sound of Music*. When a studio buys the film rights to a book, they often reserve the right to change the story, add and subtract characters, change the setting, and use a writer other than the author. In novels, authors have the opportunity to explain the inner thoughts and feelings of the characters in prose, but in a movie, thoughts and feelings must be translated into visual images. As a result, it is very different to write a screenplay, and the studio usually hires a screenwriter to adapt the novel into a film. Cabot felt a little apprehensive at first about the loss of control over her own characters, but once she heard that Disney had hired Garry Marshall, director of *Pretty Woman* and *Runaway Bride*, and Julie Andrews, she relaxed.

In August 2001, Cabot attended the premiere of *The Princess Diaries*. Although it was a little strange to see her own characters on screen, Cabot said that she felt, "the message of the story—being true to yourself, no matter what—remains the same. And Anne Hathaway is the perfect Mia—quirky and sweet—with Julie Andrews as a very regal Grandmère. And Mandy Moore as Lana and Heather Matarazzo as Lilly are perfectly cast."[2] Cabot attended the premiere dressed in a fun Betsey Johnson dress. Johnson is a hip designer, known for her outrageous fashions and color combinations. Back in Indiana, Barbara Cabot was thrilled to see her daughter's name in the credits of the movie. August was a terrific month, full of exciting moments like the premiere, but in September 2001, New York City would change forever. Cabot and her husband would face some tough decisions.

THE DESTRUCTION OF THE TWIN TOWERS

On September 11, 2001, Benjamin Egnatz left early in the morning for work at a financial firm in Manhattan, in a building across from the internationally known World Trade Center. Nicknamed the Twin Towers, the buildings dominated the New York skyline and had come to be a symbol of capitalism and American success.

At 8:46 A.M., a Boeing airplane crashed into the North Tower of the World Trade Center. Across America, people watched their televisions in horror and waited to see if the building could withstand the impact. Then, the unthinkable happened: A second plane hit the South Tower. Collapse was imminent, and the scene was terrible. People were trapped inside the buildings and inside the planes. When the Twin Towers collapsed, thousands were killed and thousands more were injured.

New York City's firefighters and police officers were at Ground Zero, the site of the destruction. They frantically dug people out and tried to lessen the destruction. Bridges into and out of the city closed down. Wireless phone trucks made it to the scene and hoped to locate people with cell phone signals. Across the world, families tried to get in touch with loved ones in New York City.

Shortly after the destruction of the Twin Towers, a plane hit the Pentagon in Washington, D.C. Then a fourth plane, which was also intended to hit Washington, crashed in an empty field in Pennsylvania. It slowly became clear that these were not accidents: The planes were used as weapons by terrorists. Passengers on the fourth plane were able to take the plane back from the terrorists and change its course. Although they could not save themselves, they were able to save the lives of other Americans. The world mourned the death of these heroes.

Cabot was awakened that morning by a phone call from a concerned friend. She watched the television with increasing horror. Like many Americans, Cabot tried to reach her husband, but cell phone lines were busy. When Egnatz saw the first plane hit, just across the street from his window, he evacuated his office and brought his co-workers home to his apartment. After hours of worrying, Cabot discovered that her husband was safe, but the couple was shaken.

The city seemed like a war zone, filled first with people who had run from Ground Zero and then filled with military vehicles. Individuals and businesses offered whatever they could to help the recovery effort: food, blood donations, money, or emotional support. For days after the devastation, flyers with photos of missing people flapped in the still-smoky wind. Egnatz's office was too close to the site, and their apartment was not far from the destruction. The couple decided to move to the Upper East Side, but even that location seemed precarious. The city that had been home for so long no longer felt safe.

In the 1-800-Where-R-You series, Cabot introduces another character with special powers: Jess Mastriani, who, after being struck by lightning, can find missing children. Above is the cover of the volume called When Lightning Strikes.

7

The Princess and the Publishers

THE EVENTS OF September 11, 2001, scarred New York City and its people both physically and emotionally. Longtime residents were uneasy in well-populated venues. People cut down on their travel. Cabot and Egnatz made the move to Yorkville, on Manhattan's Upper East Side. This area, where the couple found a much less expensive apartment, was lovely and settled, and the couple was happy in their new home. They had lived in Greenwich Village, which is famous as a young, hip haven for writers, artists, and other creative thinkers. After the move to a new apartment, Cabot made the move to work from her bed instead of from her desk.

Dressed in her pajamas, Cabot still put in an eight-hour workday; she just did it from the comfort of her bed. The old apartment had a view of the Twin Towers, and Cabot thought that if she had been at her desk during the attack, her back would have been to the window. The unprotected position unsettled her, and she moved to the bed. In an interview with the *Chicago Sun-Times*, Cabot said,

> After 9/11 I started writing in bed because we lived 20 blocks from [Ground Zero] and we lived in a high-rise. I started freaking out, because I'd think: "What if a plane was coming and I couldn't see it?" Then I started writing in my bed because then at least I had something at my back. But now I think I'm allergic to my pillows or something.[1]

Despite the terror of the attack and the disruption of the move uptown, Cabot still wrote consistently, although she wrote under several different names. For romance, she used the name Patricia Cabot; for *The Princess Diaries* and adult chick lit, she used Meg Cabot; and for her paranormal young adult novels, she wrote as Jenny Carroll. The books by Jenny Carroll included the Mediator series and the 1-800-Where-R-You series. The books shared some qualities with *The Princess Diaries*. They were each a quick read with a breezy tone and a strong female protagonist, but the strength of each girl was markedly different.

GIRLS OF A FEATHER

In the 1-800-Where-R-You series, Cabot introduces another character with special powers. This time the character is Jess Mastriani, who, after being struck by lightning, can find missing children. Cabot had the idea after she and a friend were standing under an awning that was struck by lightning. They had hoped for great powers but were disappointed. Nevertheless, the idea lingered in Cabot's mind, and she created the series. Jess, like Cabot's other female protagonists, has to use her brain to solve problems. She also has to do it against some savvy opponents, one of which is the federal government. Like Suze, the character from the Mediator series, Jess grows as a result of her power. Cabot has said that she is interested in how one outstanding characteristic can affect the character's development and social interaction.

At first, Jess tries to stay anonymous. She sees faces on milk cartons, and once she is asleep, she dreams of the missing children. By morning, she knows where the children are. Worried that she will be considered a freak, she reports the information from busy pay phones around town. The government soon discovers her whereabouts, though, and tries to force her into their service. Jess cannot tell if they want her for good or evil, and all she wants is for the publicity to go away so that she can once again think about cute boys and chat with her best friend. She also wants to protect her family from the media spotlight. Between the federal government and the media, "Lightning Girl," as she has been nicknamed, wants only to disappear. The problem is that people continue to disappear, and their loved ones come to Jess for answers.

In *Sanctuary,* the second book in the series, a neighbor asks Jess for help after Jess has sworn off using her power:

> I backed up until my calves hit the stairs to the second floor.
> When they did, I had to sit down on the first landing, which
> was only about four steps up, because my knees didn't feel
> like they would hold me up anymore.

"I don't—" I said, through lips that seemed to have gone as cold as ice. "I don't do that anymore. Maybe nobody told you. But I don't do that anymore."[2]

As in so many of her novels, Cabot's protagonist is a young woman who tries hard to become an individual, to be true to her friends and family, and to use the gifts that she has been given. Cabot planned Jess's story as a series: Over the course of five books, Jess develops from a high school girl into an accomplished woman in college. The books proved so popular that the Lifetime Channel picked up the series and called it "Missing." The series lasted for three years, but although the main character was based on the books, by the second and third season the characters and plot were very different from those Cabot had developed.

In Cabot's other paranormal series, Mediator, the main character, Suze Simon, also struggles with relationships. Cabot, unlike many authors before her, acknowledges that a girl might fall in love with a guy and still want to kiss someone else. She does not promote promiscuity by any means, but she knows that it is rarely as simple to choose a boyfriend as movies and books suggest. Suze struggles with her love for Jesse and her attraction to another young man, and she does not always win the battle, but readers see her try to rationalize her decisions.

One of Cabot's talents is her ability to mine and illuminate the psyche of young women. This has added to her popularity, and surely comes, at least in part, from the very detailed journals she kept as a teenager. Cabot declares that these journals will never see the light of day. Indeed, she has taken measures to prevent the more incriminating things from coming to light, including cutting out certain pages and putting them through the paper shredder.

Other stand-alone teen novels by Cabot feature young women who also have to decide who they are. Steph Landry, in *How to Be Popular*, must decide whether to be true to herself and the people who love her best or be a part of the popular crowd. In *Teen Idol,* Jen Greenley, the friendliest

Did you know...

Meg Cabot initially wanted a calico cat because her husband, Ben Egnatz, was fond of that variety. A friend suggested that she speak with a woman who had found a litter of abandoned kittens. Cabot picked one-eyed Henrietta, the last kitten in the litter. When she brought the cat to the vet, she learned that Henrietta was not a calico but a tortoiseshell cat, animals known to be difficult. Nevertheless, Cabot soldiered on. She brought the near-comatose cat back to the apartment, where Henrietta just lay on the floor as if she were dead. She finally perked up when Cabot put food out. The cat devoured an entire can of food in seconds and then began to climb the curtains. Since that time, Henrietta has shown a marked preference for Cabot, rather than Egnatz, although Cabot had to fight with the cat when Henrietta stole Cabot's wedding ring and hid it in her special spot behind the bed. When Cabot moved the bed, Henrietta reared up on her hind legs and bared her claws. It took three months for the two to heal the rift. Henrietta will roll over when Egnatz points, and she growls when people approach the house.

girl in school, needs to discover if her friends will still like her if they know her real opinions. In *Pants on Fire*, Kate Ellison has to decide who she really is, and whether or not she is ready to reveal that to herself, her town, and Tommy Sullivan.

Of course, all of these books represent a trend in the novel: the bildungsroman, or coming-of-age story. For these young women, the teenage years represent the most crucial juncture in their lives, the moment when they decide what kind of women they want to become. This age group has huge appeal for Cabot, but she is also interested in characters who have entered the next stage.

QUARTER LIFE CRISIS

In her chick lit, Cabot began to explore the "quarter-life crisis." This is a recent term in pop culture that refers to college graduates in their twenties, who, for the first time in their lives, have no idea what happens next. For many people, their lives from birth to age 22 are pretty standard. They attend elementary school, junior high and high school, then college. After college, though, they are faced with a multitude of choices: what to do, where to live, whom to marry, where to travel, how to pay bills, as well as college and credit card debts. The array of choices is almost limitless and can become debilitating. As a result, people settle for low-wage jobs to build a career or to give them time to figure out what they really want to do. Cabot writes chick lit like the Queen of Babble series to address this social phenomenon.

EPISTOLARY NOVELS: AN UPDATE

Cabot's Boy series is connected through a loose network of office characters linked through the newspaper publishing world. The books use one of the most contemporary incarnations of the epistolary novel. An epistle is a letter, and an epistolary novel uses the form of the letter to tell the story. The form became popular in the 1700s when an Englishman, Samuel Richardson, wrote his novel *Pamela* in the epistolary form.

Many critics believe that *Pamela* was the first novel that was ever written. Novels became tightly integrated stories that strived for realism and intimacy, as well as sentiment. In *Pamela*, a young servant girl writes letters to her parents about her time as a servant for Mr. B, who repeatedly tries to seduce her. Pamela resists him, and the man eventually comes to love her and admire her stalwart refusals. Finally, he offers her marriage, the only way that she agree to engage in a relationship with him.

In a letter to her beloved father, Pamela writes about her employer's attempts to seduce her and then dismiss her:

I said, when I could speak, Your honour will forgive me; but as you have no lady for me to wait upon, and my good lady has been now dead this twelvemonth, I had rather, if it would not displease you, wait upon Lady Davers, because—I was proceeding, and he said, a little hastily—Because you are a littlefool, and know not what's good for yourself. I tell you I will make a gentlewoman of you, if you be obliging, and don't stand in your own light; and so saying, he put his arm about me, and kissed me! Now, you will say, all his wickedness appeared plainly. I struggled and trembled, and was so benumbed with terror, that I sunk down, not in a fit, and yet not myself; and I found myself in his arms, quite void of strength; and he kissed me two or three times, with frightful eagerness.—At last I burst from him, and was getting out of the summer-house; but he held me back, and shut the door. I would have given my life for a farthing. And he said, I'll do you no harm, Pamela; don't be afraid of me. I said, I won't stay. You won't, hussy! said he: Do you know whom you speak to? I lost all fear, and all respect, and said, Yes, I do, sir, too well!—Well may I forget that I am your servant, when you forget what belongs to a master.[3]

Pamela fights back, determined to protect her virtue, one of the few things that makes her desirable as a wife. In accordance with the mores of the time, Pamela is marriageable because she is a good-looking, hardworking, and virtuous young woman. Unfortunately, she has no money or social standing, which makes her less desirable; the story ends, somewhat unrealistically, as her employer marries her because he respects her fight for her virtue. The story was meant to champion chastity. It was subtitled *Virtue Rewarded*, which suggests that a rich marriage is the reward for abstinence. Critics of the time disdained the novel for its middle-class morality, and feminist critics today are appalled at the supposed reward and the blatant sexual harassment.

Nonetheless, the romance genre has a long tradition with the epistolary novel, a tradition that Cabot updated by making the epistles into e-mails. In the first novel of the series, *The Boy Next Door,* Melissa Fuller rescues an ailing neighbor and takes her to the hospital. With her neighbor comatose, Mel takes charge of her abandoned Great Dane until the neighbor's nephew moves into her apartment to care for the dog. Unfortunately, the "nephew" is not who he appears to be. At work, Mel is in charge of the page-10 gossip columns, which update the world on the lives of various celebrities. Although Mel claims that she wants to be moved to serious news, she secretly delights, as Cabot herself does, in the Hollywood gossip. The e-mails and interoffice mail shoot across the workplace. As in her young adult novels, the heroines are surrounded by a bevy of helpful friends, ready to dispense advice and hear the dish.

In *Boy Meets Girl*, Kate Mackenzie is living with her married friends after she leaves her boyfriend of 10 years. The ex-boyfriend refuses to commit, and Kate decides to move on, although she has no idea how. At work, Kate has to fire an adored member of the staff dining room, and that staff member sues her for wrongful termination. In the midst of all of this turmoil, Kate finds herself attracted to her lawyer, a man from a wealthy family who seems to be the antithesis of what Kate wants. In this novel, as in many that address women in their 20s, it seems to be harder for women to figure out what they want than to actually get it.

In the final novel of the series, *Every Boy's Got One*, Cabot continues the epistles, but this time they come from Italy. A maid of honor and a marriage-phobic best man try to help their friends to the altar, despite their own love-hate attraction to each other. Cabot based the book on her own wedding in Italy, and the marriage phobia of the best man comes directly from Cabot's own formerly marriage-shy husband.

ORIGIN OF A GENRE: CHICK LIT

These novels fit rather neatly into a genre called chick lit. Cabot claims that genre was actually started by Richardson. She said, "I would argue *Pamela* by Samuel Richardson was, since Pamela actually balanced romance and a career, much like Bridget Jones."[4] Richardson was one of the first authors to write a book from the point of a view of a working woman who was struggling in her quest for love.

Chick lit often follows a fairly formulaic style of writing. It begins with a young woman, usually in her 20s or 30s, who tries to figure out how to achieve her career goals, and how to find the man of her dreams. A number of feminist scholars object to books of this sort because they suggest that all women care about is fashion and love. Careers are often sacrificed to achieving love in these books. Nevertheless, for Cabot, the genre is an opportunity to write fun books about women for women, although she does not intend to exclude men. In fact, she often receives fan e-mail from young men who have read her books either for fun or to learn more about the women in their lives. Romance writers like Barbara Cartland or literary writers like Jane Austen, both of whom have been a great influence on Cabot, played a major role in the genre's long history.

FEMINISM AND FEMINASTY

Cabot objects to any comments that portray chick lit as anti-feminist. As an ardent feminist, Cabot believes that women should have all of the economic, social, and personal rights that men have. Feminism began in the United States and the United Kingdom at the end of the nineteenth and the beginning of the twentieth centuries. For most historians and critics, feminists in that first wave of feminism were trying to gain contractual, political, and property rights. They believed that women should be able to enter into business deals, vote, and own property just as men did. This early wave of feminism is associated with the women's suffrage movement.

The second wave of feminism followed World War II, when women were striving to change inequality. They demanded equal pay for equal work, and they wanted to change certain cultural ideas. In Betty Friedan's ground-breaking book *The Feminine Mystique*, she objected to the idea that only marriage and children could make women feel fulfilled. Instead, she suggested that women were creative and intelligent beings who would be fulfilled by a career. In addition to the Friedan book, women fought to stop office policies that allowed men to fire women who became pregnant and similar types of sexual harassment and discrimination.

Some believe that a third wave of feminism began in the 1990s to continue the second wave and to correct some of the directions that seemed misguided. Some feminists argued that the second wave paid little attention to any women outside of the white middle and upper classes. The third wave embraced a more global perspective, and it fought for the rights of women across the world, whatever their age, creed, color, and sexual orientation.

Cabot wholeheartedly embraces feminism, and she thinks that some people have tried to make feminism into something it is not: man hating. Certain political and social groups, interested in undermining feminism and the power it affords women, have made concerted efforts to portray feminists and the movement as a man-hating militant extremist group. Certainly, as with every group, there are extremists, and there are dozens of strains of feminism. For Cabot, feminism does not preclude wearing pretty dresses, lipstick, and Jimmy Choo shoes. A feminist has the right to do that, as well as to make millions of dollars and run a company. The point is to have options. On her blog, Cabot espouses feminist writers and criticizes women who claim not to be feminists, most famously singers Gwen Stefani, Björk, and PJ Harvey. In an interview in *Vogue*, Stefani talked about the No Doubt song "I'm Just a Girl," and said that she did not realize it would be taken up as a feminist anthem. She herself denies any feminist tendencies, saying,

> The scene that I grew up in with female artists like Bikini Kill and Hole and all these more punk-rock girls, I always had the pressure of "You've got to be a feminist and you've got to hate guys. And you've got to cuss and be tough." And I was never like that. I grew up, like, a Catholic good girl. Total *Brady Bunch* family. That always kind of scared me, the pressure of having to be so cool. . . . But I kind of got over that and realized that, yes, I love to dress up and I love to wear makeup and be myself. I like being a girl; I like having a door opened for me; I like all that traditional stuff and I won't deny it.[5]

Cabot objects, as many feminists do, to the idea that feminists must hate men and dress in a manly fashion, an odd juxtaposition. In an interview with *Bust* magazine, PJ Harvey says,

> I don't ever think about [feminism]. I mean, it doesn't cross my mind. I certainly don't think in terms of gender when I'm writing songs, and I never had any problems as the result of being female that I couldn't get over. Maybe I'm not thankful for the things that have gone before me, you know. But I don't see that there's any need to be aware of being a woman in this business. It just seems a waste of time.[6]

Cabot feels that women who deny their feminism are saying, to an extent, that they should be paid less than their male counterparts, that the efforts of women who have come before them are insignificant, and that there is no societal prejudice against women. Such attitudes show a certain degree of naiveté and a lack of concern for other women. For Cabot, it just does not make sense to deny it. As a writer in the chick-lit, young adult, and romance genres, Cabot is a particularly persuasive person to argue the idea that women can be feminists and also adore romance.

Meg Cabot has long been a fan of Jane Austen, a writer who lived from 1775 to 1817. Austen paid homage to and poked fun at British society in her day; her influence is often cited by authors of modern chick lit.

8

A Chick Who
Writes Chick Lit

CABOT'S WORK FITS into a number of literary genres. One genre, chick lit, became hugely popular in both the 1790s and the 1990s. In the 1700s, the novel was just beginning to evolve into the form with which audiences are familiar today. Novels became sustained narratives, with developed characters and points of view. In addition, in the 1790s, women became educated and learned to read because of the rise of the middle class. They did not need every child to tend the farm or care for the other children; instead, there was time and money to send the children to school and see them educated. As a result of this education, women readers became a new market for fiction.

ROMANCE NOVELS AND THE UNITED STATES—
A ROMANCE

In 1794, Susannah Rowson wrote *Charlotte Temple*, which took its cue from a genre made popular by novelist Samuel Richardson. In addition to *Pamela,* Richardson wrote *Clarissa*, in which a young woman is seduced and then abandoned. Similarly, in Rowson's novel, a British military officer seduces Charlotte Temple, takes her to New York, impregnates her, and then abandons her, which leads her to madness, poverty, and eventually, death.

Seduction stories of this type might be considered early romance novels, except that the story rarely ended happily. Instead, the woman was punished in some fashion: Either she had a child out of wedlock, she was shunned, she was disowned by her family, or even all three. Nevertheless, the titillating portion of the seduction made people want to read, and the righteous punishment made the book seem morally appropriate.

Charlotte Temple became the first bona fide bestseller in the United States, which attested to the power of the female readership. According to scholar Francis W. Halsey in his 1905 introduction to the novel, *Charlotte Temple* outsold every book in colonial times and was matched in staying power only by Benjamin Franklin's *Autobiography*. Indeed, as recently as November 2007, the book made it into a *New York Times* article about the hold it still has over American readers.

Critics called Rowson's work frivolous and overly sentimental. They criticized Rowson's portrayal of the little things in a woman's life, from fashion to social class requirements. The female characters in romance novels were often stymied by their class. A woman might love a man of a higher class, but she would never be able to marry him. Even today, this kind of "social climbing" is popular in movies and on television, although the characters often move from the unpopular clique to the popular clique while they try to maintain their sense of self and dignity.

At the time, such details were thought to be beneath the notice of both men and literature. Critics accused Rowson's work of being popular tripe and a throwaway read. Interestingly, the book has never gone out of print, and it has been reprinted more than 200 times. It would seem that Rowson did something right. Nevertheless these kinds of charges plagued women writers for the next two centuries and continue to do so.

Around the same time, in the 1790s, Englishwoman Ann Radcliffe began to write gothic novels. They were filled with supernatural phenomena, brought on by actual occurrences, as well as hallucinations due to hysteria. Her book, *The Mysteries of Udolpho*, published in 1794, became a wildly popular "sensation" novel, meant to stir the senses of the reader. As Cabot did some 200 years later, Radcliffe combined the elements of horror and romance to create her novels. Victorians greatly enjoyed her work because it titillated the senses. Academics at the time, as with Rowson, dismissed the genre as a whole, although some applauded Radcliffe. Her detailed descriptions of Italy and her use of popular themes like the beautiful and the sublime appealed deeply to readers.

Radcliffe's novels certainly moved one of her readers. Novelist Jane Austen poked gentle fun and paid homage to *The Mysteries of Udolpho* in her book *Northanger Abbey*. In fact, Austen's use of Radcliffe's book was very similar to Cabot's use of popular culture. Austen employed the sensation novel and Radcliffe's popularity to educate readers about the fashion and pop culture of her day. *Northanger Abbey* also helped to introduce the comedy of manners, in which much of the conflict and the drama are derived from the conventions and social mores of the day. From proper manners in the drawing room to social status and marriage prospects, the potential for conflict was great.

Each of these writers opened a door for Cabot and other contemporary female authors. Rowson showed the publishing world that women could create huge demand in the marketplace, a lesson that has been taught again and again. Cabot's books, which have sold more than 15 million copies, also illustrate this, as they are primarily sold to girls and women. Radcliffe introduced the supernatural and the female protagonist, although Cabot would toughen up the protagonist considerably. Austen used the comedy of manners to reveal the misguided nature of particular social ideas like the subjugation of women, the conflicts based on class, and the unnecessary importance given to fashion. Cabot also examines the social issues of the day, such as premarital sex, the cult of popularity, or feminism. Each of these women added to the development of chick lit.

In a more contemporary vein, Judy Blume and Helen Fielding created opportunities for Cabot, as well. Cabot remembers when she first read Judy Blume's books at the Monroe County Public Library. Although widely read, Judy Blume's books have also been widely banned for her frankness about teenage sexuality, eating disorders, menstruation, and other "taboo" subjects. The girls in her novels were not like Nancy Drew, who had a cute car, a cute boyfriend, and an overall cute life. Instead, they struggled and they talked to God, their friends, and their diaries, as they worried about their weight, bad hair, late periods, and eating disorders. The books revealed the inner workings of young minds and, in so doing, gave a whole generation of readers books in which they might find themselves: imperfect and unsure.

In fact, Judy Blume was so influential for so many women writers that an anthology was published called *Everything I Needed to Know About Being a Girl I Learned From Judy Blume*. In the collection, 24 women writers, including Cabot, discuss what they learned from Blume's books, both as women and, in some essays, as writers. Cabot's piece talks about Blume's book *Blubber*, and the effects of bullies.

Cabot, like Blume, gets into the psyche of young women. She writes with an interior monologue that runs throughout the whole book. Readers always know what the protagonist thinks and what motivates her. A review in *Publishers Weekly* said that reading a Cabot book is like getting a note from your best friend. Cabot's characters also make tough decisions about relationships, as do Blume's characters.

In 1974, Blume published her novel *Forever*, which dealt very frankly with a young couple in love who wanted to have sex for the first time. The description was bold and detailed, which shocked many parents. As a result, the book was often banned from public libraries or lent only with special permission. Nevertheless, it comforted many young adults who wanted to know about sex and whether their feelings were normal. The book became an emotional touchstone for many young people.

Cabot, too, addresses the question of sex in a number of her books. Her characters consider the pros and cons and ultimately make their own decisions. Cabot makes sure that those decisions best reflect what the character believes is right for herself, and is careful not to moralize. In fact, different characters take different paths, but Cabot does not judge another woman's decision to have sex. In *Ready or Not: An All-American Girl Novel*, Cabot condemns the teen who calls other girls names.

BRIT LIT, CHICK LIT

Another great movement in chick lit came with the international popularity of a certain ditzy blonde who tries to make her way in London: Bridget Jones. When Fielding's *Bridget Jones's Diary* hit the market, it exploded. Everyone was talking about units of alcohol, Mark Darcy, and turkey curry buffets, and by extension, about Jane Austen. Her book *Pride and Prejudice* was Fielding's inspiration. The movie cemented that popularity and sent even more readers to the books for further delicious scenes from *Bridget Jones*. This book, often marketed in bright, fun colors, became the "beach read" of the late twentieth century. Cabot's Boy series uses a similar formula to great effect. As noted historically, the sassy female protagonist who thinks about fashion, men, and her job is often thought to be too flippant and shallow for serious literature. Critics think chick lit "dumbs down" culture, because women read chick lit instead of literature. Apparently, critics think that chick lit has nothing to teach.

As with any type of literature, there are great practitioners of the genre and there are lesser practitioners. Cabot's books show that the search for love is part of what most women want, but perhaps the bigger part is to understand what makes the main character a better, happier person. A character may embrace the very activity that she has loved all her life, as in the case of Lizzie, who works with vintage clothing in *Queen of Babble*. Another could take a chance and believe in her own talent, as Heather Wells does in *Size 12 Is Not Fat*. She does not immediately get the guy in the story; instead, she nabs a murderer and continues—ploddingly—to write her own songs. She makes a way for herself, and that

Did you know...

Cabot began a tradition the day that her first book was published. Excited to see her book on the shelves of her local bookstore, she gathered her friends together and asked them to go to the store with her. They planned to take a picture of the triumphant author with her first published book, but the bookstore had not ordered it. Cabot was crushed, but her friends decided to ask the store to order the book. Each approached the clerk separately to ask about it, so they could convince the store management that there would be a great demand should they decide to carry it. Cabot called her husband to tell him about the plan, and he asked all the people in his office to go to their local bookstores and order the book. This started a phone chain back to Cabot's mother in Indiana, all the way down to Cabot's grandmother in Florida. Since then, Cabot and her friends have preordered each new book to make certain that it will be in the bookstores. Now, of course, most bookstores carry Cabot's books and celebrate them when they debut. Cabot's friends still call her when a book comes out, just to cheer her on.

is the best kind of affirming chick lit. For some, the label *chick lit* is derogatory. Writer Curtis Sittenfield compared it to a situation in which one woman called another woman a slut. For others, the label is a source of pride.

To its credit, the genre has also caused women to talk about books again. Oprah's Book Club has certainly had a major impact on books in America, but Cabot had her own impact. In June 2001, Cabot met another young adult writer, Tamora Pierce, who writes fantasy novels with strong female protagonists. Cabot and Pierce began to talk about their childhoods and their love of reading. Each had grown up with a deep love of books, which meant escape from boredom and isolation. Yet, each author had wondered about the lack of bold independent women characters in books. It seemed that the boys had all the fun. In an interview with Young Adult Library Services, Cabot said,

> I was a sci-fi fan when I was the age of my characters. I had a real problem finding books growing up that had feisty, funny, female heroines. A lot of books for teens at that time tended to be message books about "don't have sex before you get married" or "don't get anorexia." I wanted my reading to be about being entertained, not preached to, so I turned to sci-fi and fantasy. That's where I found heroines that I could relate to and liked.[1]

In that genre, the two authors found a few heroes who excited them, and when they talked about them, the joy was contagious. Pierce came up with an idea to create a Web site where people could discuss female heroes, from politics to entertainment, with a special focus on books. Cabot named it "Sheroes," and Pierce's husband put together the site. It debuted in 2001 and quickly accumulated 500 members by the end of the first year. Now its numbers are in the thousands, and it also claims a spin-off site, Sheroes Fans.

In addition to the Sheroes site, Cabot also worked on creating her own site, MegCabot.com, at a reader's suggestion. The site began simply, but has evolved into a multi-media event. Fans can hear about upcoming events, read Cabot's blog, see a slide show of photos that feature Cabot at all ages, and print a list of her books. Cabot talks about the origin of each series and lists the books in it. On her blog, Cabot relates details about her life, her book tours, and the television shows she watches. The same breezy, friendly voice that readers find in her books is present on the blog. Cabot also has a MySpace page with an astonishing number of friends who give her well wishes, comment on her books, or ask about her cat.

Protagonist Suze Simon of the Mediator series has been seeing ghosts ever since she was a small child. Now a typical teenager, she must learn to help the ghosts who seek her out while handling the usual demands of growing up. **Shadowland** *is the first volume of the series.*

9

Beach Babe

AFTER THE TRAGEDIES of 2001, Cabot and her husband were ready for a change. They felt uneasy in New York City, and Cabot's sudden spike in income with the sale of the rights to *The Princess Diaries* changed their everyday needs. Their accountant suggested that the couple take up permanent residence in another state to cut down on the amount of income tax they needed to pay. He provided them with a list of recommended states. Florida stood out from the rest.

The island of Key West, the southernmost city and island of the continental United States, was a bohemia of sorts filled with all kinds of characters: from beach bums and fishermen to artists and salvage workers. Many famous writers also chose Key West as their homes at one point or another, including Ernest Hemingway, Elizabeth Bishop, Tennessee Williams, Judy Blume, Wallace Stevens, and Shel Silverstein. Florida seemed to have everything the couple wanted. In particular, Cabot, who does not like to drive, could ride her bike to the places she needed to go, and there would be year-round sunshine. Egnatz could cook with an abundance of fresh seafood, and Key West had all the artsy energy of their beloved Greenwich Village. The couple did not find their dream house until a few years later.

In the meantime, Cabot published books at an amazing rate. In 2002, *She Went All the Way*, *The Boy Next Door*, and *Kiss the Bride* came out, all of which were directed at adult audiences. Young adults were satisfied, as well: Cabot published *Princess in Love*, the third volume of the beloved "Princess Diaries" series, in addition to *All-American Girl*, *Safehouse*, and *Sanctuary*. It was a prolific year.

BLOGOSPHERE

In 2003, Cabot continued the frenetic pace, and she started her blog in March. Initially, she had been reluctant about the extra work, but the new venue gave her an opportunity to speak to fans en masse. Cabot and Dr. Michele Jaffe answer questions submitted by readers about life, love, and writing in her diary section. Cabot reviews movies, television shows, and books, and provides links to other sites of interest. She also posts tour information and sneak peeks at upcoming books. Although she started with a single entry in March, the number has grown to screen upon screen of gossip, advice, and anecdotes.

The year also brought changes for Cabot's husband, Benjamin Egnatz. After September 11, he realized that his true passion was food. It was the act of creation that interested him, not his dissertation. When his dissertation adviser passed away, Egnatz finally lost all interest in his graduate studies. He turned to food and to the French Culinary Institute.

Cabot spent June in Connecticut, where she finished the sixth book in the Mediator series and enjoyed nature in between bouts of record-breaking rain. She recalls that she saw some deer while there, a pair that may have been the carriers of the tick that infected Cabot with Lyme disease. In July, she got word that Disney had passed on the script for *All-American Girl*, which they had purchased the film rights. The option reverted to Cabot and she decided to hang on to the film rights for the forseeable future.

In July 2001, Cabot promoted Lifetime's new show, *Missing,* which took its premise and some of its characters from her 1-800-Where-R-You series. After a more relaxed August, Cabot headed to Italy to complete research for her book *Every Boy's Got One*. Research went well and the trip was a dream.

TICK BITE!

Part of the dream was troubled, however. Cabot had not felt well; instead of the whirling dervish who wrote multiple books in a year, Cabot became lethargic and forgetful. Her wrists were sore, and she slept late into the day. She avoided exercise at all costs and did not even feel like writing. It seemed that regardless of what she ate, or how much she slept, Cabot could not find her characteristic verve. In December 2003, she went to her doctor for a routine checkup. A few days later, her doctor called with the news: Blood tests revealed that Cabot had Lyme disease. Somehow the author, who never ventures into the woods, had contracted the disease, which Cabot attributed to the month in Connecticut, where she often saw deer.

Most cases of Lyme disease in North America are contracted as a result of a deer tick bite. After the tick bites, a bull's-eye rash usually appears and some patients get flu-like symptoms. If Lyme disease is treated quickly, antibiotics can usually clear it up, but if the disease has progressed, the symptoms become much worse. They can include muscle and joint pain, exhaustion, a stiff neck, arthritis, and certain cognitive defects (problems with thinking). The medicine would cause sensitivity to light, so Cabot decided not to take it until the end of her Christmas holiday in Key West. That meant she would still be ill during her January book tour, but it was too much to ask for the sun-loving author to give up those days by the pool.

Luckily, Cabot's treatment began to work quickly. She had to follow a modified diet: She was forbidden sugar, flour, and alcohol, so she ate lean meats, cheese, nuts, and fresh produce. Cabot found that she lost weight in the first month of treatment, partly because of the food she ate and partly because of her newfound energy. She bounded out of bed, biked, walked through town, and swam. She

Did you know...

Cabot has fans all over the world. Readers can visit Web sites created for readers in the United Kingdom, Hungary, France, the Netherlands, Poland, and Sweden. At those sites, you can see pictures of all of her books and view the different covers and different titles. Cabot generally does one international and one national book tour a year. The publishing company sets up those tours based on the interest shown by particular bookstores. Cabot goes wherever there is the greatest interest.

felt energized and alive, and she was able to conduct her promotional *Boy Meets Girl* tour in January with minimal problems.

BOOK CLUB

In May 2004, Cabot started her first book club, MegCabot bookclub.com. Cabot often takes the suggestions of her fans quite seriously, and the Cabot book club began in exactly that way. Based on a suggestion by reader Allison Mishkin and the hard work of her Web master, Janey Lee, Cabot started the book club to talk about young adult books with her fans. She did not talk only about her own books. Instead, she introduced fans to her favorite books, some of which were contemporary, and some of which were from her childhood.

Cabot put a few restrictions on the site. First, the books had to be fun and entertaining. She did not want to reproduce Oprah's Book Club, where the majority of the books seemed to be about terrible things that had happened to people. She wanted things to be kept light. Second, before they posted comments, fans had to pass a quiz, which kept younger siblings and other mischievous parties from posting on the board. Cabot also brought in the author to join in the talk with readers, which gave them a chance to meet and question the author in a virtual chat room. Cabot thought about how much she would have liked to talk with a live author as a young adult and decided to add that feature.

The club began with Susan Juby's *Miss Smithers,* where Juby herself weighed in on the conversation. Mary Stewart's *The Moonspinners* followed. Stewart had written some of the romantic suspense novels that Cabot read as a child, as well as a series based on the King Arthur legend (as did Cabot). In addition, Stewart's heroines were smart women, who were able to help themselves, and her heroes were fairly ordinary men thrust into extraordinary situations. Clearly, Cabot and Stewart shared a point of view in regard to characterization. Their heroines act, rather than being acted upon.

The book club was a great success, and Cabot loved chatting with her fans. In May, Egnatz graduated from the French Culinary Institute, which fulfilled a lifelong dream. Cabot helped to support him in his dream as he had supported her writing.

In June, she finished a draft of *Ready or Not,* the second book in the "All-American Girl" series. In this book, Samantha Madison struggles to decide whether or not to have sex with her boyfriend, David. In *All-American Girl,* the first book, Samantha saved the life of the president and then began to date his son. As a reward for her bravery, she is asked to serve as a teen ambassador for the United States. The position will allow her to communicate the teenage point of view to the government.

In this particular book, the job becomes more important than a few press appearances, and she is forced to think about what she stands for as the teen ambassador. Will she support the "Save the Family" plan of the president, her boyfriend's father, or will she follow in the rabble-rousing footsteps of her liberal coworker, Dauntra? During a televised conference to support the Save the Family plan, Sam finds herself on the brink of a great decision that will affect her, as well as a nation of teenagers:

> "But that's . . . that's wrong!" I couldn't believe I was the only one in the room who seemed to think so. I looked down at Kris and the other kids from Adams Prep. "Don't you get it? Do you hear what he's saying? This Return to Family thing . . . it's all a crock! It's a trick! It's a . . . a . . . "

Suddenly, Dauntra popped into my head. Dauntra, who *couldn't* return to her family, because she'd been thrown out by them. Dauntra who questioned authority—so much so, she was willing to get arrested for it.[1]

Regardless of her choice, Samantha has to figure out what she believes for herself, and whether or not she has the guts to defend her beliefs and stand by the consequences of making them public.

In July, Cabot stayed in Key West and found the bike of her dreams. Purple Heat had flames painted on it and a wide seat. It made traveling around Key West fun and stylish. She also took a short book tour of Indiana, where she discovered that Bloomington, Indiana, had named a day in her honor. July 31, 2004, was deemed Meg Cabot Day, and Cabot herself was there to celebrate it. The summer passed pleasantly, with work and holiday celebrations, but soon the weather would change.

HURRICANE MAGNET

Fall weather in Florida meant hurricanes. During hurricane season, it was necessary to board up the house; nail down shutters; gather candles, matches, and blankets; and prepare for the worst. This time it was particularly bad, with four major hurricanes that hit Florida. Winds were more than 120 miles per hour; large portions of the state were flooded. It seemed as though Florida, which they had chosen as a safe haven from terrorism, was being terrorized by storms instead. Cabot and Egnatz spent a good portion of the fall either preparing for or recovering from bad weather. Cabot did get a break from hurricane season during her English book tour, where she traveled across England to give talks in bookstores and meet fans.

By the holidays, Cabot was tired. Her family had visited for Thanksgiving, she faced looming deadlines, and Christmas was coming. She decided to look at other people's decorations rather than put up her own. Then, she finally completed a manuscript in December. In January, Cabot headed to another book tour, this one for her third book in the Boy series, *Every Boy's Got One*.

Cabot had also worked on a draft of the Disney film, *Ice Princess*. Karen Glass, the executive with whom Cabot had worked on *The Princess Diaries*, contacted Cabot to see if she wanted to write a movie about a girl figure skater. A movie buff of the first order, Cabot thought it would be fun. She concocted a plot about a female hockey player with many brothers and a father who is the hockey coach. The family moved so her older brother could train for the Olympics. Callie (later renamed Casey) got a job at the concessions stand at the rink and met lots of figure skaters, and then she learns to figure skate on the sly. In the meantime, a slimy figure-skating boy seduces her, but Callie returns her affections instead to the hot Zamboni driver who happens to be in a band. Cabot went through multiple rewrites before the studio called in a different screenwriter. Little of the original plot remains. In the film, Callie becomes Cassie, a physics whiz, and rather than living in a house full of men, she lives with her mother. Cabot is proud, however, that the Zamboni-driving hottie stayed in the final film. Like Mia Thermopolis before her, Callie/Cassie becomes a princess on her own terms, in keeping with the Cabot philosophy.

CONSOLIDATION

When Cabot began to write, she had three different publishers: one for romance, one for paranormal young adult fiction, and one for *The Princess Diaries* and her adult chick-lit series. Originally, with Simon & Schuster, Cabot found that her creativity was a bit stifled. She had planned an eight-book series for the 1-800-Where-R-You series. Simon & Schuster did not buy her next four-book proposal, so the story ended right in the middle. In the Mediator series, Simon & Schuster cited poor sales and cut her off after four books.

In 2005, HarperCollins bought the rights to many of her books. Her new publisher allowed her a sixth and final book in the 1-800-Where-R-You series. Luckily, HarperCollins also agreed to let her finish the Mediator series with two more books. To support that decision, they bought the rights to the first four books and reprinted them under Cabot's real name. With the success of *The Princess Diaries* and the exposure from the movies, Cabot was a bankable name. With that name, she was able to take even more risks, such as vid lit (videos that deal with books and authors) and manga. Cabot was embracing the world of her readers, the international world of technology.

Meg Cabot and Ben Egnatz moved to Key West, Florida, in 2004. A few years later, they found and purchased their dream house (above), where they live now.

10

New
Horizons

THE YEAR 2005 began with a cold and a book tour, fairly typical for Cabot. In February, she sold her first house in Key West and bought a new one. *The Princess Diaries* got a facelift and became pinker and more marketable. The publishers took their cue from chick-lit marketing, where they grouped the category by color and cute covers. Cabot supported these decisions.

Cabot also gave her Web site a makeover. Inspired by a hardworking reader, Cabot created a team to improve the look of the Web site and to consolidate the blog and the book club into one single site. Now, readers can view the blog, the book club, fun facts, biographies, and pictures from the same original site. The site contains archived blogs and advice from Cabot and Jaffe. The look of the site is more colorful and more sophisticated. The menu also offers a breakdown of Cabot's work based on age, as well as updates on tours and publication information.

As usual, the good was mixed with the not so good. More hurricanes ravaged Key West. In fact, Hurricane Katrina and Hurricane Rita, which left New Orleans in shambles,

Did you know...

When Cabot and Egnatz moved into their first house in Key West, Florida, locals told them it was haunted. Allegedly, an older woman named Mary who used to live there had stuck around. Past owners complained of mysteriously opened windows and doors, missing or moved possessions, and doorbells that seemed to ring without the help of human hands. Cabot does not believe in ghosts, although when she was an assistant dorm manager at New York University, one of her residents claimed to have seen a ghost in her room. When Cabot sent her to counseling, a colleague informed her that the resident's description of the ghost matched that of a student who had died in her room in the 1970s. Years later, Cabot had to contend with her own ghost, whom Cabot blamed for her unexplained cravings for gingersnaps.

both blew through Key West, although they were nothing compared to the devastation visited upon New Orleans and Mississippi. In typical Key West fashion, many residents chose to ride out the hurricanes. They boarded up windows and pulled pets inside. When the rain cleared, they waded through the water to any place with electricity and gathered for hurricane parties. Despite the general good feeling in the community, Cabot and her husband were tired of angry cats and downed power lines. The Midwest was beginning to look like a haven during hurricane season. In 2007, the couple bought an old farmhouse in Indiana, which they refurbished like their other houses with a state-of-the-art, left-handed kitchen for Egnatz.

In their Key West home, for the first time in years, Cabot embraced Christmas. She put up lights, placed poinsettias on the front step, and decorated a white sparkly tree with ornaments and a pink flamingo topper. Nevertheless, it was not all fun that Christmas season. After a long and full life, Cabot's maternal grandfather died, and Cabot returned to Indiana for the funeral. She had been close to her grandfather. As with so many of her loved ones, he became a model for some of the characters in her books, particularly Mia Thermopolis's maternal grandfather and Steph Landry's grandfather in *How to Be Popular*.

FOLLOW THAT EDITOR!

In 2006, Cabot opted for a major change. Her longtime editor, Abigail McAden, with whom she had worked since 1998, moved to Scholastic Books, where she would head their new line of teen books. Cabot knew that the partnership was good for her writing, so she followed her. Writers often follow their editors, or move to new publishers for higher royalties, better promotions, or a new genre of writing.

Scholastic was receptive to Cabot and her book proposals, which outline two new trilogies aimed at teen readers. Airhead, the first trilogy, is about the world of high fashion, and Cabot describes it as a dramedy. In Abandon, her second upcoming series, she returns to her paranormal writings with a book that borrows from the myth of Persephone. Persephone was a Greek goddess, daughter of Demeter, or Mother Earth. Hades fell in love with her and took her to the underworld. Demeter was bereft without her daughter; she plunged the world into winter, and refused to let anything grow until her daughter was returned. Unfortunately, Persephone had already eaten six seeds of the pomegranate in the underworld, which meant that she could only be allowed to return to the earth for six months out of the year. In this way, the Greeks explained seasons. No doubt Cabot will create compelling relationships between mother and daughter, young woman and abductor.

For the younger crowd, ages 8 to 12, Cabot is writing her Allie Finkle series. She hopes that this will keep younger readers and their parents satisfied until they grow into her teen books.

After her move from HarperCollins, Cabot decided to consolidate her Web sites. HarperCollins had maintained the sites, but Cabot had to take over the site herself when she switched publishers. She chose to bring it all together, which made it easier to manage and less expensive. In January, *Avalon High* debuted at No. 3 on the *New York Times* bestseller list for children's chapter books. Cabot was thrilled, but one of her greatest thrills came later that year.

For years, Cabot had waited for her books to be banned. She felt that it meant that an author had taken a risk and made a difference. Like Judy Blume, her literary role model, she wanted to spread the word about things that people rarely spoke about publicly, even if the information was necessary and useful. In *Ready or Not*, Cabot's main character, Samantha, thinks about having sex with her boyfriend for the first time. Sam's sister, Lucy, offers her advice and she also purchases safe sex products for her. Cabot believes that it is better to talk about sex, rather than preach abstinence to help young women make informed choices, whether they choose to wait or to pursue a sexual relationship. For her, the point is that young women are empowered by knowledge. Some librarians and parents did not agree with her. Her books either were taken off library shelves or held for special release restricted by age.

THE NEXT STEPS

In 2007, it was an optioning free-for-all for Cabot. Many major Hollywood players wanted to buy the options for a number of her books. In July, the Disney Channel optioned the rights of *Avalon High* for a potential television movie, and in August, MTV purchased *How to Be Popular.* In September, Julia Pistor, the producer of the *Lemony Snicket* and *Spiderwick Chronicles* movies, optioned the Mediator series, and in October, the Queen of Babble series sold to the independent film company responsible for movies that include *Proof, Boys Don't Cry*, and *Nicholas Nickleby*. The next few years have the potential to make Meg Cabot a huge multimedia influence, as she explores other genres in addition to the movies.

HarperCollins, Cabot's old publisher, had brokered a deal with TokyoPop, a publisher of Japanese anime comic books called manga. The collaborators had tried many authors, but they decided to start with Cabot's continuation of the Avalon High series. The first of the trilogy, *The Merlin Prophecy,* debuted in summer 2007. Cabot was able to choose the artist with whom she worked. After she saw the sketches of multiple artists, Cabot found that Jinky Coronado saw the characters just as she did. As a former illustrator herself, Cabot felt it was important that she think the artist's work was far superior to her own. With Coronado, she had little doubt. In October 2007, her choice was confirmed when *Avalon High: Coronation: The Merlin Prophecy* was nominated for a Young Adult Library Services Association (YALSA) Great Graphic Novel award.

In addition to the manga series, Cabot also pursued vid lit, in which she created a video of a day in her life, which readers can access from her Web page. These videos might take on a slice of life for the author, or even a note about a book or character. She also sends text messages and short stories, via cell phone, to devoted readers as part of a marketing strategy, and believes that they will appreciate and understand this approach. She has also created Meg-A-Readers, an elite group of readers who receive advance copies and special news that they can spread to friends. This is similar to the Cabot ambassadors that she tried in England, and the strategy worked.

In July, *Jinx* was published. For readers who love her earlier paranormal series, *Jinx* seems to be a perfect fit. The story of a teenage witch who inherited her powers from a long line of witches is based on Cabot's own family. A very distant ancestor was actually burned at the stake in England for witchcraft. Readers may think that the story is about

Cabot, but in fact, the family witch seems to be Cabot's mother, Barbara. Born on Friday the 13th, Barbara Cabot's longtime nickname is Jinx. *Queen of Babble in the Big City* also hit shelves. The book continues with Lizzie Nichols and her new love as they begin their life together in New York. As of November 2007, the third Heather Wells novel, *Big Boned*, hit the shelves to great success.

THE CABOT WAY

Cabot has made a career from being herself, as she writes in her own teen-inspired voice about her own dreams and experiences. She refused to be cowed by bad reviews and repressive workshops. Instead, she continued to try because she loved what she was doing. Perhaps that is Cabot's supernatural power: the ease and fearlessness with which she creates stories and characters that appeal to girls from age six to adulthood. She is sure to have a book that contains a smart heroine who struggles to stay true to herself and to her friends. Thankfully, with her prolific rate of publication, readers always have one more book to anticipate.

With Cabot, there is always more to come. In the near future, fans can expect her two new trilogies, her children's books, more books in the Princess Diaries series, and many more blog entries. Readers will never have to wait long for Cabot to get the itch again, to start playing the "What if?" game, and to begin a new story that empowers and entertains.

CHRONOLOGY

1967 Meggin Patricia Cabot is born in Bloomington, Indiana, on February 1.

1970 Meg's brother Matthew is born.

1972 Meg's brother Nick is born and the Cabots adopt him two months later.

1980 The Cabots move to California during Vic Cabot's sabbatical year, where teacher Dan Gotch encourages Meg to write; Meg begins to baby-sit for Susan Gubar and continues until 1985.

1983 Cabot meets Benjamin Egnatz for the first time at a party.

1985 Cabot enters Indiana University as an art major.

1989 Cabot moves to New York City with her boyfriend.

1991 Cabot completes her degree from Indiana University and earns a B.A. in art. She begins to work at New York University as an assistant residence hall manager.

1993 Meg Cabot marries Benjamin Egnatz in Italy; Cabot's father dies of cancer.

1996 Laura Langlie becomes Cabot's agent.

1998 Cabot's first book, a historical romance, is published; she writes under the name of Patricia Cabot; she begins writing the Mediator series.

2000 *The Princess Diaries* is published by Harper Collins; Cabot options the story to a movie company and quits her job at New York University; the first book of the Mediator series is published; Cabot begins to work for Pocket Books, the publisher of her romance novels.

2001 *The Princess Diaries* opens in theaters; the Twin Towers are destroyed; Cabot meets Tamora Pierce and the two create the Sheroes Web site to talk about female heroes in literature and life; Cabot creates her own Web site through HarperCollins.

2002 Cabot and Egnatz move to the Upper East Side.

2003 Cabot contracts Lyme disease and starts her blog.

2004 Egnatz attends the French Culinary Institute; Cabot starts the Meg Cabot book club; Bloomington, Indiana, proclaims July 31, 2004, to be Meg Cabot Day, in honor of their native daughter; Cabot and Egnatz buy a house in Key West, Florida.

2005 HarperCollins buys the rights to reissue the Mediator series; Cabot completes that and the 1-800-Where-R-You series and to rerelease and complete the Mediator series; Cabot and Egnatz buy a new house in Key West and refurbish it.

2006 *Ready or Not: An All-American Girl Novel* gets banned in select areas; Cabot's maternal grandfather dies; Cabot begins work on the Airhead trilogy.

2007 Cabot leaves HarperCollins and follows her editor to Scholastic Books; Cabot and Egnatz buy a home in Indiana; Cabot begins to advertise for the Allie Finkle tween series; Cabot publishes her first manga.

NOTES

Chapter 1

1 Meg Cabot, interview by the author, e-mail, Bellefonte, Pa., December 2006.

Chapter 2

1 Barbara Cabot, interview by the author, e-mail, Bellefonte, Pa., February 2007.

2 Meg Cabot, interview by the author, e-mail, Bellefonte, Pa., December 2006.

3 Ibid.

4 Ibid.

5 Ibid.

Chapter 3

1 Meg Cabot, interview by the author, e-mail, Bellefonte, Pa., December 2006.

2 Ibid.

3 Ibid.

4 Meg Cabot, interview by the author, e-mail, Bellefonte, Pa., February 2007.

Chapter 4

1 Barbara Cabot, interview by the author, e-mail, Bellefonte, Pa., February 2007.

2 Meg Cabot, "Avon's Little Black Book," *Size 14 Is Not Fat Either*. New York: Avon Trade, 2006.

3 Meg Cabot, interview by the author, e-mail, Bellefonte, Pa., February 2007.

4 Barbara Cabot, interview by the author, e-mail, Bellefonte, Pa., February 2007.

5 Meg Cabot, interview by the author, e-mail, Bellefonte, Pa., February 2007.

6 *Boston Herald* 27 July 2001.

Chapter 5

1 Meg Cabot, *Every Boy's Got One.* New York: Avon Books, 2005, p. 227.

2 Frederick Hecht, William C. Shield Jr. et al, eds., "Squamous Cells," *Webster's New World Dictionary*. New York: Wiley, 2003.

3 Barbara Cabot, interview by the author, e-mail, Bellefonte, Pa., February 2007.

4 Ibid.

5 Laurie Gold. "Patricia Cabot: Cross-Genre Phenomenon." All About Romance: The Back Fence for Lovers of Romance. July 23, 2001. www.laurielikesbooks.com/Cabot.html.

6 Meg Cabot, *Shadowland*. New York: Harper Teen, 2000, p. 31.

Chapter 6

1 Meg Cabot, *The Princess Diaries*. New York: Harper Trophy, 2000, p. 190.

2 Cathy Sova. "Meet Author Meg Cabot." The Romance Reader. May 16, 2001. http://www. theromancereader.com/cabot.html.

Chapter 7

1 Dawn Reiss, "Babble On," *Chicago Sun-Times* 24 June 2007.

2 Meg Cabot, *Sanctuary*. New York: Simon & Schuster, 2002, p. 12.

3 Samuel Richardson. *Pamela, or Virtue Rewarded*. November 29, 2007. http://www.gutenberg. org/catalog/world/readfile?fk_ files=12050&pageno=12.

4 Meg Cabot, interview by the author, e-mail, Bellefonte, Pa., March 2007.

5 Joathan Van Meter. "The First Lady of Rock." Style.com. Originally appeared in the April 2004 issue of *Vogue*. November 29, 2007. http://www.style.com/vogue/ feature/032204/page2.html.

6 Christina Martinez, "Polly's Phonic Sphere," *Bust Magazine* (Fall 2004).

Chapter 8

1 Paula Brehm-Heeger, interview with Meg Cabot, *Young Adult Library Services*, Fall 2006, p. 11.

Chapter 9

1 Meg Cabot, *Ready or Not: An All-American Girl Novel*. New York: Harper Teen, 2005.

WORKS BY MEG CABOT

1998 *Where Roses Go Wild*

1999 *Portrait of My Heart*

1999 *An Improper Proposal*

2000 *A Little Scandal*; *The Princess Diaries*; *Shadowland*; "The Christmas Captive," novella in the anthology *A Season in the Highlands*

2001 *Ninth Key*; *When Lightning Strikes*; *The Princess Diaries, Volume II: Princess in the Spotlight*; *Code Name Cassandra*; *Educating Caroline*; *Lady of Skye*; *Reunion*; *Darkest Hour*

2002 *Safe House*; *The Princess Diaries, Volume III: Princess in Love*; *Kiss the Bride*; *Nicola and the Viscount* (reissued in 2005); *Sanctuary*; *All-American Girl*; *The Boy Next Door*; *She Went All the Way*

2003 *Haunted*; *Victoria and the Rogue* (reissued in 2005); *The Princess Diaries, Volume IV: Princess in Waiting*; *Princess Lessons: A Princess Diaries Book*; *The Princess Diaries, Volume IV and a Half: Project Princess*; "Girl's Guide to New York Through the Movies" in *Metropolis Found*; "Kate the Great" in *13: Thirteen Stories that Capture the Agony and Ecstacy of Being Thirteen*, ed. James Howe

2004 *Boy Meets Girl*; *The Princess Diaries, Volume V: Princess in Pink*; *Perfect Princess: A Princess Diaries Book*; *Teen Idol*; "Party Planner" in *Girls' Night In*

2005 *Every Boy's Got One*; *Twilight*; *The Princess Diaries, Volume VI: Princess in Training*; "Connie Hunter Williams, Psychic Teacher," in *Friends: Stories About New Friends, Old Friends, and Unexpectedly True Friends*, edited by Ann M. Martin and David Levithan; *Ready or Not: An All-American Girl Novel*; *The Princess Present: The Princess Diaries, Volume VI and a Half*; *Holiday Princess: A Princess Diaries Book*

2006 *Avalon High*; *Size 12 Is Not Fat*; *The Princess Diaries, Volume VII: Party Princess*; "Reunion," in *Girls' Night Out*;

Sweet Sixteen Princess: A Princess Diaries Book, Volume VII and a Half; *How to Be Popular*; *Queen of Babble*; *Size 14 Is Not Fat Either*

2007 *Valentine Princess: A Princess Diaries Book*; *Missing You*; *The Princess Diaries, Volume VIII: Princess on the Brink*; "The Exterminator's Daughter," in *Prom Nights From Hell* "Cry, Linda, Cry: Judy Blume's *Blubber* and the Cruelest Thing in the World" in *Everything I Needed to Know About Being a Girl I Learned From Judy Blume*, ed. Jennifer O'Connell; "Allie Finklestein's Rules for Boyfriends," in *Shining On*; *Pants on Fire*; *Queen of Babble in the Big City*; *Avalon High 2: Coronation*, three-book manga series, Book 1: *The Merlin Prophecy*; "Ask Annie" in *Midnight Feast*; *Jinx*; *Big Boned*

2008 *The Princess Diaries, Volume IX: Princess Mia*

POPULAR BOOKS

THE ALL-AMERICAN GIRL SERIES

Punkster Samantha Madison becomes a reluctant hero after saving the president's life. Now, Sam has become a teen ambassador and the girlfriend of the president's art-loving son, David. In the two novels published thus far, Sam has to deal with her popular older sister, decisions regarding sex with her boyfriend, and her public profile as teen ambassador.

THE MEDIATOR SERIES

Protagonist Suze Simon has been seeing ghosts ever since she was a small child. Now a teenager who lives in California, she must learn to help the ghosts who seek her out, as well as handle a growing crush on the attractive ghost who has inhabited her house for more than 100 years. At the same time, she also has to handle her best friend, her new brothers, and her new confidante, a fellow ghost mediator.

THE 1-800-WHERE-R-YOU SERIES

Teenager Jess Mastriani gets struck by lightning, and as a result, she develops the ability to see missing people. Jess feels a responsibility to protect her family from the media, and she also thinks she has to work for the federal government, which has decided that Jess's unique power could help them in a number of ways. In the midst of it all, Jess tries to create a relationship with Rob, the cute older boy from the wrong side of the tracks.

THE PRINCESS DIARIES SERIES

Mia Thermopolis is just an average, environmentally conscious nerd, daughter of a single mom, and would-be girlfriend of her best friend's brother—until she gets the news that she is, in fact, a European princess. Over the course of nearly a dozen books, Mia navigates the rough waters of first love, princess-hood, a new sibling, school bullies, and a romance between her teacher and mother.

THE HEATHER WELLS SERIES

Heather Wells, former teen pop-singing sensation, has fallen on hard times. Her father is in jail, and her mother has stolen all of her money and run off. Her former boyfriend, a fellow pop idol, has left her for her arch nemesis. His brother, the man she really loves, has offered her his home, but not his heart. Still, all is not lost: Heather is writing her own songs; she is in close proximity to Cooper, the man of her dreams; and she has a job as an assistant residence hall manager. Unfortunately, residents in her hall are dying and only Heather can solve the mystery.

THE QUEEN OF BABBLE SERIES

Vintage clothes nut Lizzie Nichols has almost graduated from college, and she decides to head to England to spend the summer with her English boyfriend. When the trip turns into an epic disappointment, she crosses the pond to find her best friend, who is staying in France. Once there, Lizzie falls for Luke, son of a French vintner. She talks constantly, which gets her into trouble, whether she is in France, or in later books, New York.

THE AVALON HIGH SERIES

Elaine Harrison (Ellie) is new in Annapolis, and she finds herself interested in the local teen hottie, Will Wagner, but it is more than a crush. The two seem to be unusually connected. As events unfold, their story begins to bear an unsettling resemblance to the legend of King Arthur.

POPULAR CHARACTERS

FATHER DOMINIC

Father Dominic is a priest and principal of Suze's school. Like Suze, he is a mediator. Unlike Suze, he chooses to talk to ghosts and tries to resolve their issues by peaceful, nonaggressive means. He teaches Suze a great deal about the responsibilities of being a mediator.

KATIE ELLISON

Katie of *Pants on Fire* is accustomed to telling lies. She has held onto a big one since the seventh grade. Katie runs for Quahog Princess, kisses the wrong boy, and lives in fear that the return of her old friend Tommy will lead to some uncomfortable moments of truth.

GRANDMÈRE

Grandmère, Queen of Genovia, is an officious, mannered, smoking grandmother to Mia Thermopolis. She teaches her granddaughter to behave like a princess with special attention to antiquated etiquette. Both affectionate and maddening, she is dedicated to her duties as both Genovian royalty and grandparent.

JENNY GREENLEY

Jenny is the protagonist of *Teen Idol*. A gregarious girl, she is a friend to everyone in the school, regardless of cliques. Part of what makes her so beloved is that she rarely tells people when they are wrong. She is also the anonymous columnist for the school paper, and because of her ability to keep a secret, she is asked to keep the biggest secret the school has ever known, a secret that has the potential to come between her and her best friend.

ELAINE HARRISON

Elaine, known as Ellie, is the daughter of two medievalists. Her parents are so obsessed with Arthurian legend that they named their daughter after Lady Elaine of Astolat, known to many as the Lady of Shallot. The lady in question was made famous by a Tennyson poem of the same name. Ellie has moved to Annapolis because her parents are on sabbatical. She finds herself obsessed with Will Wagner, floating around her pool, and breaking records at track meets.

JESSE

Jesse is the nineteenth-century cowboy/ghost/hottie who haunts Suze Simon's room. Suze is in love with him, but the two have to contend with his past before they can ever think about being together.

STEPHANIE LANDRY

Stephanie is the protagonist of *How to Be Popular*. In her high school, if someone does something clumsy, they are pulling "a Steph Landry." Eager to be rid of her outcast status, Steph creates a plan by which she will become popular. In her plan, she must look and act certain ways, which alienates her from her true friends.

LUCY MADISON

Lucy is Samantha's perfect older sister. She is beautiful, popular, and trendy, unlike Sam. Nevertheless, Lucy comes through for her sister with fashion advice and help with her love life. She is dating Jack, the brooding artist who Samantha thinks she might also like.

SAMANTHA MADISON

Samantha is the girl who saved the president! But before her new-found fame, she dyed all of her wardrobe black because she was "in mourning for our generation." Politically aware and environmentally concerned, she has frizzy red hair, a skinny frame, and a talent for art. She is also dating the president's son and trying to handle her fame and her new love.

JESSICA MASTRIANI

Jessica, the main character in the 1-800-Where-R-You series, has special powers; she can locate missing people. She gained her power after being struck by lightning. Unfortunately, her new power also brought her to the attention of the federal government, who wants to study Jess and use her powers for their own reasons, not all of which are good.

LILLY MOSCOVITZ

Lilly is Mia's best friend. Often sarcastic, sometimes painfully so, Lilly hosts a public access cable television show, *Lilly Tells It Like It Is,* where she focuses on controversial issues like global warming and cafeteria wrongs. She is also Michael's sister.

MICHAEL MOSCOVITZ

Michael is a senior while Mia is a freshman. He is brother to Lilly, band member, scientific genius, and the crush of Mia's life.

LIZZIE NICHOLS

Lizzie, recent almost-college graduate, is the *Queen of Babble*. She talks constantly, a trait that often leads to trouble. She is crazy about fashion and likes to restore vintage garments.

KRIS PARKS

Kris is Samantha Madison's former best friend. In Sam's absence, Kris has become a self-righteous, boy-chasing, popular-crowd elitist. She is only nice to girls who are thin, blond, and expensively dressed.

CATHERINE SALAZAR

Catherine is Samantha Madison's best friend after her return from Morocco. Unlike Kris Parks, she still likes Sam and does not mind her all-black ensembles. Catherine herself can only wear skirts due to a zealously religious mother.

SUZANNA (SUZE) SIMON

Suze is the protagonist of the Mediator series. Suze can talk to people who have not settled peacefully into death. As a mediator, she is meant to help them resolve their life issues so they can move on to the next world. Unfortunately, Suze is inclined to punch first and talk later. She lives in California with her mother, stepfather, three stepbrothers, and a handsome ghost who inhabits her bedroom.

PAUL SLATER

Paul is also a mediator, but he has powers that Father Dominic does not have. He comes from a family of mediators, although he does not respect his lineage. Tall, dark, and gorgeous, he tries to win Suze's affections from Jesse. Suze is attracted to him, but she wisely questions his ethics.

MIA THERMOPOLIS

Fourteen-year-old Mia, protagonist of *The Princess Diaries*, suddenly gets big news: She is a princess! That still does not change the fact that her mother is dating one of her teachers and that Mia's hair is a frizzy mess. Mia lives with her free-spirited artist mother and is a little bit in love with her best friend's brother. She has to figure out how to be the best friend, best daughter, best princess, and best person she can be.

A. WILLIAM WAGNER

A. William is the quarterback at Avalon High, a National Merit Finalist, and president of the senior class. Tall, dark, and attractive, he is also thought to be the reincarnation of King Arthur, sent back to the world to conquer evil. He and Ellie have an inexplicable bond between them.

LANA WEINBERGER

Lana is Mia's arch nemesis. She is a popular cheerleader who likes to put other people down. Mia sees her as the embodiment of all that is evil about popularity.

HEATHER WELLS

Heather, former pop star, is now the assistant residence house coordinator at a college in New York City. While she works on new material that shuns her pop past, she also deals with murders in the dorms, weight gain, and living with her ex's sexy older brother.

ROB WILKINS

Rob is a grit, an outsider, a juvenile delinquent. Still, he has black curly hair, pale blue-gray eyes, and broad shoulders. Jess meets him in detention and falls in love with him. Rob is older and tries to steer clear of her, worried that she will get him into trouble. She continues to drop by the garage where he works, and he helps her locate missing children and evade the FBI.

MAJOR AWARDS

1999 *An Improper Proposal* wins the *Romantic Times* Reviewers Choice Award for Best British Isles Historical Romance.

2001 *The Princess Diaries* wins the American Library Association Award for both Reluctant Readers Selection and Best Book. It also wins the New York Public Library Teen Books for the New Millenium citation, as well as a Book Sense Pick, an IRA/CBC Young Adults' Choice and an Evergreen Young Adult Book Award. *The Princess Diaries II* wins an ALA Quick Pick for Reluctant Young Adult Readers and a New York Public Library Pick, as does *Princess Diaries Volume III*.

2002 *All-American Girl* is listed by the New York Public Library as a Book for the Teen Age. It is also selected as an IRA/CBC Young Adults' Choice, a Book Sense Pick, an Evergreen Young Adult Book Award winner in Washington State, and an ALA Quick Pick for Reluctant Young Adult Readers.

2003 *Safe House* wins an Edgar Allen Poe Award nomination in the best young adult category voted by the Mystery Writers of America.

2003 *The Princess Diaries* is voted "one of the nation's 100 best-loved novels" by the British public as part of "The Big Read" sponsored by the BBC. *The Princess Diaries IV* is listed again by the New York Public Library.

2004 *The Princess Diaries V* is named an amazon.com customer favorite and listed as an IRA/CBC Young Adults' Choice. *Teen Idol* is listed by the New York Public Library.

2006 *Avalon High* is listed on the Texas Lone Star Reading List and the New York Public Library List of Books for the Teen Age. *How to Be Popular* is also listed by the New York Public Library.

Branch, Shelly. "Twisting Phrases? Shut-Up!" *Wall Street Journal*, May 1, 2003, p. A-1.

Brehm-Heeger, Paula. Interview with Meg Cabot. *Young Adult Library Services*, Fall 2006, p. 11.

Cabot, Barbara. Interview with the author. E-mail. Bellefonte, Pa. February 2007.

Cabot, Meg. "Avon's Little Black Book." *Size 14 Is Not Fat Either*. New York: Avon Trade/Harper Collins, 2006.

———. *Every Boy's Got One*. New York: Avon Books/HarperCollins, 2005.

———. Interview with the author. E-mail. Bellefonte, Pa. December 2006, February 2007, and March 2007.

———. *The Princess Diaries*. New York: Harper Trophy/HarperCollins, 2000, p. 190.

———. *Ready or Not: An All-American Girl Novel*. New York: Harper Teen/HarperCollins, 2005.

———. *Sanctuary*. New York: Simon Pulse/Simon & Schuster, 2002, p. 12.

———. *Shadowland*. New York: Avon Books/HarperCollins, 2000, p. 31.

Gold, Laurie. "Patricia Cabot: Cross-Genre Phenomenon." All About Romance: The Back Fence for Lovers of Romance. July 23, 2001. www.laurielikesbooks.com/Cabot.html

Hecht, Frederick, William C. Shield Jr. et al, eds. "Squamous Cells." *Webster's New World Dictionary*. New York: Wiley, 2003.

Martinez, Christina. "Polly's Phonic Sphere." *Bust Magazine*, Fall 2004.

Reiss, Dawn. "Babble On." *Chicago Sun-Times* June 24, 2007.

Richardson, Samuel. *Pamela, or Virtue Rewarded*. November 29, 2007. http://www.gutenberg.org/catalog/world/readfile?fk_files=12050&pageno=12.

Sova, Cathy. "Meet Author Meg Cabot." The Romance Reader. May 16, 2001. http://www.theromancereader.com/cabot.html.

Tom, Kristina. "Living Her Dream." *The Strait Times* (Singapore) June 11, 2006.

Van Meter, Jonathan. "The First Lady of Rock." Style.com. Originally appeared in the April 2004 issue of *Vogue*. November 29, 2007. http://www.style.com/vogue/feature/032204/page2.html.

FURTHER READING

"Meg Cabot." *Authors and Artists for Young Adults*, Volume 50. Gale Group, 2003. Reproduced in *Biography Resource Center*. Farmington Hills, Mich.: Thomson Gale, 2006.

Web Sites

Author Profile: Meg Cabot
http://www.teenreads.com/authors/au-cabot-meg.asp

Meg Cabot Book Fest '05
http://rs7.loc.gov/today/cyberlc/feature_wdesc.php?rec=3758

Meg Cabot: Official Web Site
http://www.megcabot.com

Meg Cabot's Interview: BBC, Onion Street
http://www.bbc.co.uk/schools/communities/onionstreet/liveguests/interviews/megcabot.shtml

The Official MySpace of Author Meg Cabot
http://www.myspace.com/meg_cabot

Popgurls.com: 20 Questions with Author Meg Cabot
http://www.popgurls.com/article_show.php3?id=516

Scholastic Kids: Allie Finkle
http://www.scholastic.com/alliefinkle/

Sheroes
http://www.sheroescentral.com

Sheroes Fans
http://www.sheroesfans.com

PICTURE CREDITS

page:

10: Courtesy Meg Cabot

14: Courtesy Meg Cabot

18: Courtesy Meg Cabot

22: Courtesy Meg Cabot

26: Courtesy Meg Cabot

28: Courtesy Meg Cabot

33: Courtesy Meg Cabot

37: Courtesy Meg Cabot

40: Courtesy Meg Cabot

47: AP Images/ Tina Fineberg

50: Time & Life Pictures/ Getty Images

56: Courtesy Meg Cabot

60: Used by permission of HarperCollins Publishers.

67: Disney Enterprises, Inc./ Photofest

72: Jupiter Images. Photo by SMPhotography.

86: Library of Congress, photo # cph 3c03529

96: Cover art © 2005 by Paul Oakley. Cover design by Sasha Illingworth. Cover © by HarperCollins Publishers, Inc. Photo by SMPhotography.

106: Courtesy Meg Cabot

INDEX

1-800-Where-R-You series, 35, 74, 105
  books in, 31, 74–76
  television series, 76, 99

Abandon series, 110
Airhead trilogy, 110
Alexander, Lloyd, 31
All-American Girl, 98–99
  series, 102–103
Allie Finkle tween series, 110
amelioration, 13
American Library Association, 69
American Society for Prevention of Cruelty to Animals (ASPCA), 34
Andrews, Julie, 69–70
Anthony, Piers, 31
Asimov, Isaac, 31
ASPCA. *See* American Society for Prevention of Cruelty to Animals
Austen, Jane, 82
  Northanger Abbey, 89–90
  Pride and Prejudice, 92
Autobiography (Franklin), 88
Avalon High, 110
  awards for, 112
  manga, 112
  rights for, 111
Avon publisher, 68

Becca (*How to Be Popular*)
  inspiration for, 35
Big Boned, 15, 113
Bishop, Elizabeth, 98
Björk, 83
Bloomington, Indiana
  hometown, 20, 23–24, 29, 37, 53, 70, 103
Blubber (Blume), 91

Blume, Judy
  Blubber, 91
  influence of, 31, 90, 98, 111
  Forever, 91
Boy Meets Girl, 81, 101
Boy Next Door, The, 80–81, 98
Boy series, 92
  office characters in, 78–81, 101, 104
Branch, Shelley, 13
Bridget Jones's Diary (Fielding), 92
Brownhouse production company, 66
Bust magazine, 84

Cabot, Barbara Mounsey (mother), 19, 70, 93, 113
  death of husband, 55
  family, 20–21, 24–25, 27, 29, 32, 36, 41–42, 45, 62
  illustrator, 21, 46
  love life, 63–64
Cabot, Matthew (brother)
  childhood, 21, 23–24
Cabot, Meg
  and animals, 24, 39, 59, 77
  awards, 69, 112, 126
  birth, 20
  blog, 15–16, 21, 24, 30, 34, 39, 58, 83, 95, 98, 107–108
  childhood, 11–12, 17, 20–27, 29–37
  chronology, 114–115
  education, 17, 27, 30–31, 33, 36, 41–45, 64
  journals, 31, 33, 76
  and Lyme disease, 99–100
  marriage, 51–55, 61, 81
  philanthropy, 34

values and influences on, 21, 25, 29–31, 82, 111
works by, 118–119
Cabot, Nick (brother)
childhood, 21–24
Cabot, Patricia. *See* Cabot, Meg
Cabot, Vic (father), 19, 25
death, 55, 58, 61–62, 64
illness, 54–55
influence of, 54
professor, 20–21, 29, 38, 41, 57
Callallo (journal), 58
Campaign to End Fistula, 34
Carroll, Jenny. *See* Cabot, Meg
Cartland, Barbara, 82
CeeCee (Mediator series)
inspiration for, 35
Charlotte Temple (Rowson), 88–90
Chicago Sun-Times, 74
chick lit
adult, 74, 104
critics of, 92, 94
marketing, 107
origin of, 81–82, 87, 90
popularity of, 87, 92–94
quarter-life crisis in, 78–82
and romance, 85, 88–92
Christopher, John, 31
Cinderella Affair, 34
Clarissa (Richardson), 88
Collins Living Learning Center, 43
Condé Nast, 46
Contardi, Bill, 66
Cooper, Susan, 31
Cosby, Bill, 19

Danzinger, Paula, 31
Desperately Seeking Susan (film), 41
Disney Channel, 111

Egnatz, Benjamin (husband), 39, 44, 93
and animals, 77
and cooking, 98–99, 102
dating, 48–49

influence of, 58, 62
marriage, 51–54
meeting, 38
and September 11, 2001, attacks, 70–71, 73, 97–98
epistolary novels, 78–81
Every Boy's Got One
Holly in, 53, 81
tour for, 99, 104
Everything I Needed to Know About Being a Girl I Learned From Judy Blume
"Cry, Linda, Cry: Judy Blume's Blubber and the Cruelest Thing in the World" in, 91

fans
lessons learned, 16
Father Dominic (Mediator series)
peaceful mediator, 57
Feminine Mystique, The (Friedan), 83
feminism, 36–37, 90
history of, 82–85
scholars of, 82
Fielding, Helen, 90
Bridget Jones's Diary, 92
Forever (Blume), 91
Franklin, Benjamin
Autobiography, 88
French Culinary Institute, 99, 102
Friedan, Betty
The Feminine Mystique, 83
From the Black Hills, (Troy), 44

Gem (cat), 24
Giuliani, Rudy, 45
Glass, Karen, 104
Gotch, Dan, 30
gothic novel, 89
Grandmère (The Princess Diaries series)
film portrayal, 69–70
Gubar, Susan, 38
The Madwoman in the Attic, 36

Halsey, Francis W., 88
HarperCollins publishers, 68, 105, 110–111
Harvey, PJ, 83–84
Hathaway, Anne, 13, 69–70
Heather Wells (Heather Wells series), 113
    books in, 14–15
    solving mysteries, 43, 93
Heather Wells series, 113
    fraternity boys in, 43
Hemingway, Ernest, 98
Henrietta (cat), 24, 77
Hilton, Paris, 13
How to Be Popular, 35, 77, 109
    mathematical awakening in, 38
    rights for, 111

Ice Princess (film), 104
Improper Proposal, An, 62
Indiana University, 64
    education at, 39, 41–43
    father at, 20–21, 38–39, 41
    Greek systems at, 42

Jackson, Michael, 13
Jaffe, Michele, 98, 108
Jeff Herman's Guide to Agents, Editors, and Publishers, 58
Jenny Greenley (*Teen Idol*)
    and popularity, 77–78
Jesse (Mediator series)
    relationship with Suze, 76
Jess Mastriani (1-800-WHERE-R-YOU series), 35
    ability to see missing people, 74–76
    nickname, 75
    publicity, 75
    and Rob, 31
Jinx, 112–113
Johnson, Betsey, 16, 70
Juby, Susan
    Miss Smithers, 101
Junipero Serra Mission School, 30

Kate Mackenzie (*Boy Meets Girl*), 81
Katie Ellison (*Pants on Fire*), 78
Key West, Florida
    home in, 25, 100, 103, 107–108
    hurricanes in, 103–104, 108–109
    move to, 97–98
Kiss the Bride, 98

Lady of Skye, 63
Lana Weinberger (The Princess Diaries series), 70
Langlie, Laura
    agent, 58, 66, 68
Laurie Likes Books, 55
Lee, Janey, 101
Leguin, Ursula K., 31
L'Engle, Madeline, 31
Lifetime Channel, 76, 99
Lilly Moscovitz (The Princess Diaries series), 70
    inspiration for, 35
    and popularity, 65
Little, Brown and Company, 68
Little Scandal, A, 62
Lizzie Nichols (Queen of Babble series), 92
London, Stacey, 13
Lucy Madison (All-American Girl series), 111
Lyme disease, 99

Madonna, 41
Madwoman in the Attic, The (Gubar), 36
manga, 16, 112
Marshall, Garry, 69
Mary Poppins (film), 69
Matarazzo, Heather, 70
McAden, Abigail, 109
Mediator series, 35, 99, 105
    inspiration for, 57–58
    relationships in, 76
    setting of, 30
    writing of, 74
Meg-A-Readers, 112
Meg Cabot book club, 101–103, 107

Meg Cabot Day, 103
Melissa Fuller (*The Boy Next Door*), 80–81
Merlin Prophecy, The, 112
Mia Thermopolis (The Princess Diaries series), 13, 109
    film portrayal, 69–70, 104
    mother, 64
    nerd, 65
    and popularity, 65
    royal blood, 65–66
    self-consciousness of, 64–65
Mishin, Allison, 101
Missing (TV show), 76, 99
Miss Smithers (Juby), 101
Moonspinners, The (Stewart), 101
Moore, Mandy, 70
Mourning Doves (Troy), 44
MTV magazine, 46
MySpace.com, 16
Mysteries of Udolpho, The (Radcliffe), 89–90

Nancy Drew series, 90
New York City, 38
    destruction of the twin towers, 70, 73–74, 97
    move to, 45–46
New York Times, 88
New York University
    work for, 14–15, 46, 48, 68, 108
No Doubt, 84

Oprah's Book Club, 94, 101

Pamela (Richardson), 79–81, 88
Pants on Fire, 78
Pierce, Tamora, 16
    fantasy novels, 94
Piston, Julia, 111
Planned Parenthood, 46
Pocket Books, 63
Portrait of My Heart, 62
Pretty Woman (film), 69
Pride and Prejudice (Austen), 92
Princess Diaries, The, 74, 107, 113
    audio books, 69

    awards for, 69
    Genovia in, 65–66
    film production, 13, 16, 66, 69, 104
    inspiration for, 64
    popularity in, 64–65
    publication, 15, 69, 105
    rejection of, 15, 66
    success of, 69, 97, 105
    writing of, 64
Princess Diaries, Volume II: Princess in the Spotlight, The
    audio books, 69
Princess Diaries, Volume III: Princess in Love, The, 98
Princess Diaries, Volume IV: Princess in Waiting, The
    tour for, 34
Prom Nights From Hell
    "The Exterminator's Daughter" in, 36
Publishers Weekly, 91

Queen of Babble, 92
    rights to, 111
Queen of Babble in the Big City, 113

Radcliffe, Ann
    The Mysteries of Udolpho, 89–90
Ready or Not: An All-American Girl Novel, 92, 102
    banned, 111
Richardson, Samuel
    Clarissa, 88
    Pamela, 79–81, 88
Rob Wilkins (1-800-WHERE-R-YOU series)
    relationship with Jess, 31
Rowson, Susannah
    Charlotte Temple, 88–90
Runaway Bride (film), 69

Safe House, 98
Samantha Madison (All-American Girl series)
    hero, 102–103
    and Save the Family plan, 102
    and sex, 111

Sanctuary, 75, 98
Scholastic Books
  switch to, 109–110
Seinfeld (TV show), 13
September 11, 2001, terrorist attacks
  aftermath, 97–98
  events of, 70–71, 73
Sheroes Web site, 16, 94–95
She Went All the Way, 98
Silverstein, Shel, 98
Simon & Schuster publishers, 105
Sittenfield, Curtis, 94
Size 12 Is Not Fat, 14
Size 14 Is Not Fat Either, 14–15
Sound of Music, The (film), 69
Stefani, Gwen, 83–84
Stephanie Landry (*How to Be Popular*), 109
  being true to self, 77
  payroll in, 38
Stevens, Wallace, 98
Stewart, Mary, 102
  The Moonspinners, 101
St. Martin's Press, 62
Straits Times, 68
Suze Simon (Mediator series), 35
  fistfights, 57–58
  and ghosts, 57
  growth, 75
  relationships, 76

Teen Idol, 77–78
themes
  boys, 31–32, 35–36, 76
  of female friendship, 26, 35, 76, 78, 81
  finding oneself, 74–78, 91, 93
  girl power, 32, 62–63, 74–75, 92, 94, 102
  love, 92

popularity, 34, 64, 77–78, 90
premarital sex, 90–92, 111
quarter-life crisis, 78–82
sneaking out, 35
social issues, 90
vampires, 36
Tina Hakim Baba (The Princess Diaries series)
  and boys, 35
  inspiration for, 35
TokyoPop, 112
Tommy Sullivan (*Pants on Fire*), 78
Troy, Judy
  From the Black Hills, 44
  Mourning Doves, 44
  West of Venus, 44

Viewpoint Bookstore, 37
Vindication on the Rights of Women, A (Wollstonecraft), 63
Viswanathan, Kaavya, 68
Vogue, 84

Wall Street Journal, 13, 44
Walt Disney Pictures, 66, 68–69, 99
West of Venus (Troy), 44
What Not to Wear (TV show), 13
When Lightning Strikes
  romance in, 31
Where Roses Go Wild, 62
Whiting Writing Award, 44
William Morris Agency, 66
Williams, Tennessee, 98
Wollstonecraft, Mary
  A Vindication on the Rights of Women, 63
World War II, 82

Young Adult Library Services, 94

ABOUT THE AUTHOR

CAMILLE-YVETTE WELSCH is a writer and teacher who lives in Bellefonte, Pennsylvania. She studied English, creative writing, and philosophy as an undergraduate at West Chester University and the University of Leeds, and she earned an M.F.A in Poetry from Pennsylvania State University. Her work has appeared in *The Writer's Chronicle, Barrow Street, Mid-American Review, Red Cedar Review, The Women's Review of Books, Calyx, Small Spiral Notebook,* and *To the Fishhouse*. Welsch is a stringer for *Foreword Review* and *The Centre Daily Times*, as well as a senior lecturer in English at Pennsylvania State University and a grant writer.